Alternative Education in the 21st Century

Thank You!!
Wendy!!

Karen Hlady

Alternative Education in the 21st Century

LAP LAMBERT Academic Publishing

Impressum / Imprint
Bibliografische Information der Deutschen Nationalbibliothek: Die Deutsche Nationalbibliothek verzeichnet diese Publikation in der Deutschen Nationalbibliografie; detaillierte bibliografische Daten sind im Internet über http://dnb.d-nb.de abrufbar. Alle in diesem Buch genannten Marken und Produktnamen unterliegen warenzeichen-, marken- oder patentrechtlichem Schutz bzw. sind Warenzeichen oder eingetragene Warenzeichen der jeweiligen Inhaber. Die Wiedergabe von Marken, Produktnamen, Gebrauchsnamen, Handelsnamen, Warenbezeichnungen u.s.w. in diesem Werk berechtigt auch ohne besondere Kennzeichnung nicht zu der Annahme, dass solche Namen im Sinne der Warenzeichen- und Markenschutzgesetzgebung als frei zu betrachten wären und daher von jedermann benutzt werden dürften.

Bibliographic information published by the Deutsche Nationalbibliothek: The Deutsche Nationalbibliothek lists this publication in the Deutsche Nationalbibliografie; detailed bibliographic data are available in the Internet at http://dnb.d-nb.de. Any brand names and product names mentioned in this book are subject to trademark, brand or patent protection and are trademarks or registered trademarks of their respective holders. The use of brand names, product names, common names, trade names, product descriptions etc. even without a particular marking in this works is in no way to be construed to mean that such names may be regarded as unrestricted in respect of trademark and brand protection legislation and could thus be used by anyone.

Coverbild / Cover image: www.ingimage.com

Verlag / Publisher:
LAP LAMBERT Academic Publishing
ist ein Imprint der / is a trademark of
AV Akademikerverlag GmbH & Co. KG
Heinrich-Böcking-Str. 6-8, 66121 Saarbrücken, Deutschland / Germany
Email: info@lap-publishing.com

Herstellung: siehe letzte Seite /
Printed at: see last page
ISBN: 978-3-659-35021-4

Abstract

The purpose of this study was to explore paradigms, policies and practices governing alternative education in the central Vancouver Island region. I sought whether current alternative education dimensions, models and pedagogies were aligned with 21st Century learning principles set forth by the BC Ministry of Education. I interviewed key informants and approached this study with an Interpretivist qualitative research design grounded in Phenomenological principles. Findings were generally congruent with the literature regarding defining, describing and understanding alternative education. Suggestions included redefining success and using relevant criteria to evaluate program efficacy and student achievement. Successful alternative education characteristics and features were highlighted and compared to the 21st Century learning paradigm. Preliminary findings indicated similarities between the two educational philosophies. Recommendations included using successful alternative programs as models to implement 21st Century learning in mainstream schools. Future research should include student, teacher and parent voices regarding alternative education delivery models, services and evaluation.

KEY WORDS: alternative education, alternative school, alternative program, alternative student, educational philosophy, evaluation, 21st Century learning, Vancouver Island.

Table of Contents

Abstract.. ii

Table of Contents iii

List of Tables.. viii

List of Figures ix

Acknowledgments x

Dedication xi

Chapter One: Introduction 1

    Background 1

    Situating Myself in the Study: Theoretical Stance and Professional Values 2

    Introducing the Clientele: Students in Alternative Education..2

    Purpose..5

    Objectives...5

    Research Questions..5

    Scope of the Study 6

    Definition of Terms 6

    Significance of the Study 9

    Thesis Overview 9

Chapter Two: Literature Review...11

    History...11

        Recent history. 13

    Philosophy, Purpose and Typology...14

Philosophy. 14

Purpose. 15

Typology. 17

Student Profile 20

Risk factors. 21

Disabilities and designations. 24

Protective factors. 25

Relationships and school climate. 26

Resilience. 27

Alternative Programs 28

Program models. 28

Curriculum. 29

Pedagogy. 30

Integrated-community programs. 33

Characteristics. 35

Assessments and intervention strategies. 41

Entrance and exit criteria. 41

Flexible attendance policies. 43

Funding. 43

Facilities and site location. 44

Evaluations 45

Failed return to mainstream. 47

BC Ministry of Education Policy 47

Alternative education policy. 48

21st Century Learning...49

Chapter Summary...49

Chapter Three: Methodology..51

Definition of Terms..52

Methodology: Qualitative Research Design..54

Specific Methods..56

Participant Selection: Sampling and Recruitment..57

Sampling strategy. 57

Recruitment approach. 57

Data Collection, Organization and Analysis..58

Data collection. 58

Data organization. 59

Data analysis...59

Delimitations and Limitations..60

Delimitations 60

Limitations 60

Authenticity, Credibility and Trustworthiness..61

Ethical Considerations 63

Summary..64

Chapter Four: Findings..65

Introducing the Participants 65

Understanding Alternative Education...67

Alternative education philosophies...68

Theories into Practice 72

v

Purpose of Alternative Education...74

Introducing the Students 75

    Risk factors..75

    Student designations. 78

Systemic Failures...79

    Stigma. 82

Provincial Policy 84

Understanding Alternative Education Summary..85

Evaluating Alternative Education..86

Leadership Responsibilities 86

    Advocacy..86

    Funding. 88

    School Climate. 90

    Staffing...91

Goals, Graduation Plans and Transitions..97

    Learning plans. 98

    Evergreen certificate. 99

    Post-secondary transitions...100

Participants Reflections on Outcome and Process 101

    Student success and program efficacy. 103

Evaluating Alternative Education Summary..105

21st Century Learning and Alternative Education 106

Alternative Education History..106

Alternative Education Features and 21st Century Learning 107

Advisement system. 110

Flexibility, autonomy and personalized learning. 112

Curriculum, pedagogy and experiential learning. 114

Community partnerships. 116

21st Century Learning and Alternative Education Summary 118

Findings Summary..118

Chapter Five: Discussion 120

Understanding Alternative Education...121

Closing Thoughts on Understanding 124

Evaluating Alternative Education...125

Concluding Evaluations 129

Comparing Alternative Education and 21st Century Learning.................................130

Comparing Paradigms Conclusions..133

Strengths and Limitations of the Study..134

Strengths..134

Limitations 134

Recommendations 134

Future Research 138

Final Reflection 138

APPENDIX A 159

List of Tables

Table 1: Recommendations 137

List of Figures

Figure 1: Starfish analogy (Google images)...70

Figure 2: Maslow's hierarchy of needs (Google images).........................74

Acknowledgments

Thank you to my Circle of Courage™: Toresa Crawford for your guidance, editing and unconditional support; Laura Bisaillon for your superior editing skills and advice; Catherine Etmanski for your sound council; Heather Sanrud for your encouragement, faith and understanding; my dear friend Stephen Leblanc for everything else; and William Leung, my life raft and steadfastly supportive partner: Your sacrifices and unwavering support made this degree a reality. Of course, ultimate thanks go to Dr Carolyn Crippen for your guidance and patience, Dr Tatiana Gounko for your support and finally, Vivian McCormick for keeping me administratively on track, in spite of myself.

Dedication

To the youth I have known over the years, your resilience has fueled my fire, and to the youth care practitioners and alternative educators I have worked with, your dedication, humour and spirit have filled my soul. Thank you for the relationships: I am a better person for having known you.

Chapter One: Introduction

Background

For some young people, school is the only place that is safe and stable, where there might be a trusting and supportive adult, and where they can get connected to other social supports. Therefore, education programs that address the complex social and educational needs of at-risk and high-risk students are necessary to ensure they have the appropriate tools and social supports to navigate a smooth transition into adulthood. (Smith et al., 2007, p. 6)

Over the past half century, alternative education programs have emerged in response to the inability of mainstream schools to meet the needs of all students. Atkins (2008) noted that "alternative schools generally serve a variety of students with an agreed on characteristic—the students are at risk" (p. 345). Alternative schools have been attempting to connect and engage at-risk students within small educational learning communities. Kelly (1993) remarked that thousands of students across North America have been suspended, referred to alternative education programs and expelled from mainstream schools. Is this a result of student failure or systemic atrophy? Are schools flailing and failing to meet the needs of their students? (Fallis & Opotow, 2003) School principals referred disruptive students to alternative education programs once they were identified as being "at-risk of school failure" (Atkins, 2008, p. 345). Successful alternative schools responded to the needs of their students with flexibility while offering a range of educational models driven by various purposes (Raywid, 2001; Zweig, 2003).

This chapter situates the researcher, provides an overview of the research design including purpose, objectives and specific research questions, introduces the clientele and delineates the scope and significance of the study. The

1

literature review presents the history of alternative education, its philosophies and typologies, details the student profile, program characteristics, curriculum and pedagogy, while the methodology chapter expands on the research design. The final chapters present the findings in chapter four and concluding discussion and recommendations in chapter five. To begin, I share some background that has inspired me to conduct this study.

Situating Myself in the Study: Theoretical Stance and Professional Values

I have worked with vulnerable youth and families for nearly two decades and have been influenced by traditional Pacific North West Indigenous wisdom; a reflection of my life on Vancouver Island. I have worked in and around alternative education as a residential child care worker, foster parent, youth and family support worker and volunteer in youth camps. I have also had the privilege of servicing alternative schools as a youth addictions outreach counsellor. My career continues to center on providing holistic services to at-risk adolescents, a cornerstone of my practice. My professional credo is grounded in child and youth care, local Indigenous philosophies and social justice principles.

Introducing the Clientele: Students in Alternative Education

Alternative education students are youth who have not been successful in mainstream school settings. Often, these students were profiled as at-risk of school failure and came from socio-economically disadvantaged families where mental health and addiction issues were common place. Smith et al. (2007) described students who attend alternative education programs as at-risk youth.

Most students were referred to alternative programs by their mainstream school. Scholarly literature, professional journals, and government reports have consistently used demographic risk factors to describe students in alternative schools. These factors included poverty, ethnicity, family status, mental and physical health (Aron, 2006; Aron & Zweig, 2003; Lange & Sletten, 2002; Tissington, 2006). Behavioural indicators such as short attention span, reactivity and disengagement were noted in hindsight (Platt, Case & Faessel, 2006; Wood, 2001). Academic indicators such as poor work habits, low assignment turn out, lack of comprehension or ability to problem solve, and learning disabilities (Van Acker, 2007) were also used to describe students attending alternative programs.

Students in alternative programs present a range of abilities and capacities including varying levels of literacy, learning disabilities as well as academically capable students who have suffered bouts of instability, tragedy, mental and physical health issues at some point in their schooling (D'Angelo & Zemanick, 2009; Jeffries, Hollowell & Powell, 2004). Many students have been mandated to attend alternative programs (Atkins, 2008). Tissington (2006) described these students as "at-risk of dropping out, delinquent or disruptive, disabled, medically fragile, low achievers, pregnant or young parents, truant, and suspended or expelled" (p. 20). Van Acker (2007) warned that "many of these children have not been identified as displaying an educational disability; thus, they are not eligible for special education services" (p. 6).

Researchers cited risk factors such as substance use and abuse, sexual, physical and emotional abuse, pregnancy and/or parenting, mental health issues, unstable homes and poverty as impeding students' ability to engage in school (Carswell, Hanlon, O'Grady & Watts, 2009; Guerin & Denti, 1999; Johnston, Cooch & Pollard, 2004; Kubic, Lytle & Fulkerson, 2004; Lehr & Lange, 2003; Lehr, Tan & Ysseldyke, 2009; McGee, 2001; Nicholson & Artz, 2008; Wood, 2001). Developmental issues, learning disabilities and other diagnoses often accompanied students in alternative programs (Fuller & Sabatino, 1996; Nicholson & Artz, 2008; Platt, Casey & Faessel, 2006; Wood, 2001) including Fetal Alcohol Spectrum Disorder (FASD) (Watson, Westby & Gable, 2007),

3

Emotional Behavioral Disorder (EBD) (Bullock & Gable, 2006; Fitzsimons-Hughes & Adera, 2006; Flower, McDaniel & Jolivette, 2011; Foley & Pang, 2006; Gorney & Ysseldyke, 1992), and Attention Deficit Hyperactivity Disorder (ADHD) (Schnoes, Reid, Wagner & Marder, 2006).

The most notable demographic difference demarking American from Canadian students in alternative programs was their ethnicity (Lange & Sletten, 2002; Kleiner, Porch & Farris, 2002; Smith et al., 2007). American alternative schools housed more African-American and Latino students (Kleiner, Porch & Farris, 2002), whereas alternative schools in British Columbia serviced more Caucasian students than Aboriginal or other ethnic minorities overall (Smith et al., 2007). However, Aboriginal students, ethnic minorities and lower income youth are over-represented in urban alternative schools in comparison to the general school population.

Kellmayer (1995) reported alarming youth statistics from the Children's Defense Fund, illustrating "the social disintegration of the past two decades" (p. 5) in the United States. For example, some of the statistics included:

- every 8 seconds an American child drops out of school;
- every 47 seconds a child is abused and neglected;
- every 7 minutes an adolescent is arrested for a drug offense;
- teen suicide is at an all-time high;
- teen abortion is at an all time high. (p. 5)

Although listing demographic information and risk factors might provide important information about alternative students' backgrounds, barriers and challenges, these indicators fail to explain *how* to re-engage students in school. San Martin and Calabrese (2011) argued that "too often, alternative school students are viewed from a deficit based lens" (p. 111), fostering the stigma of school failure. Perhaps an examination of the educational system would shed some insight as to why certain students are not successful in mainstream school

4

and subsequently get referred to alternative education programs. Kellmayer (1995) commented that "These troubled young people needed *comprehensive programs* to address their problems – not simplistic, get-tough solutions" (p. x, *emphasis in original*).

Purpose

Having now been introduced to alternative schools' main clientele, this study pursues a further understanding of alternative education. Specifically, the purpose of this study is to explore paradigms, policies and practices governing alternative education in central Vancouver Island. I am looking to correlate current alternative education dimensions, models and pedagogy to the BC Ministry of Education's most recent educational paradigm shift: 21st Century personalized learning.

Objectives

My overarching objective is to unearth successfully implemented paradigms, philosophies and practices. I am looking to provide evidence supporting alternative education's claim that this is a credible, legitimate and viable educational pathway for students who are not successful in mainstream school. I also intend on contributing to the scholarly literature on alternative education, offering Vancouver Island's unique voice and expertise to this conversation.

Research Questions

After much deliberation, I chose to organize my queries, thoughts and subsequent findings according to the following research questions:

1) How is alternative education defined, described and understood, in contrast to mainstream public education?

2) How does one measure student success and evaluate program efficacy in alternative schools?

3) What existing approaches and/or theoretical models make alternative education viable within the 21st Century Learning paradigm?

Scope of the Study

Given the vastness of the literature and research spanning these topics, I narrowed the scope of this study to include issues specific to alternative education in the central Vancouver Island region. This study provides a common understanding of alternative education, its philosophy, purpose, and service delivery models. This study also discusses *whose needs* alternative programs are designed to meet. Alternative education is recognized as an integral part of the current educational system. This study examines, in part, whether it is the students' or system's needs that are being met. Findings are expected to elucidate the effective implementation of successful practices in alternative schools and programs within the context of the BC Ministry of Education's 21st Century Learning paradigm. However, exploring the impact of this paradigm in mainstream settings across the province is well beyond the scope of this study. These findings are intended to reflect the lived experiences of participants and the students they represent.

Definition of Terms

The following definitions contextualize the concepts of alternative education, school and program. Aron and Zweig (2003) buttressed these definitions against that of regular school. Several American researchers (Aron & Zweig, 2003; Bullock, 2007; Cable, Plucker & Spradlin, 2009; Jones, 2011; Magee-Quinn, Poirier, Faller, Gable & Tonelson, 2006) reiterated the US Department of Education's (2002) definition of alternative school as "a public elementary/secondary school that addresses needs of students that typically

6

cannot be met in a regular school, provides non-traditional education, serves as an adjunct to a regular school, special education or vocational education" (Table 2, p. 14, as cited in Aron, 2006, p. 3).

Aron and Zweig (2003) relied on the Iowa Association of Alternative Education's (IAAE) definitions to distinguish nuances:

o <u>Alternative Education</u>: the study or practice of implementing alternative schools or programs. Public alternative education serves to ensure that every young person may find a path to the educational goals of the community. Alternative schools and programs focus on what they can offer the student, not on what problems the student has had in the past. Alternative education is a vital component of the total educational system.

o <u>Alternative School</u>: an established environment apart from the regular school. With policies and rules, educational objectives, staff and resources designed to accommodate student needs, an alternative school provides a comprehensive education consistent with the goals established by the school district. Students attend via choice.

o <u>Alternative Program</u>: an established class or environment within or apart from the regular school. An alternative program is designed to accommodate specific student educational needs such as work-related training, reading, mathematics, science, communication, social skills, physical skills, employability skills, study skills, or life skills.

o <u>Regular School</u>: an established environment designed to provide a comprehensive education to the general populace to which assignment of students is made more on the basis of geographical location than unique education need. (Aron & Zweig, 2003, p. 23)

A few years later, Aron (2006) redefined alternative education as:

Schools or programs that are set up by states, school districts, or other entities to serve young people who are not succeeding in a traditional public school environment. Alternative education programs offer students who are failing academically or may have learning disabilities, behavioural problems, or poor attendance an opportunity to achieve in a different setting and use different innovative learning methods (p. 6).

The BC Ministry of Education defined alternative education as "programs that meet the special requirements of students who may be unable to adjust to the requirements of regular schools" (as cited in Smith et al., 2007, p. 7). The McCreary report (Smith, 2007) does not define, but describes alternative programs as those "that address the complex social and educational needs of at-risk and high-risk students are necessary to ensure they have the appropriate tools and social supports to navigate a smooth transition into adulthood" (p. 6). Aron and Zweig (2003) made the distinction between schools and programs, whereas Canadian sources did not. However, the literature used the terms interchangeably, as will I.

At-risk students were characterized by their risk factors, school designations and related socio-economic side effects in the literature. Tissington (2006) described alternative students as being "at-risk of dropping out, delinquent or disruptive, disabled, medically fragile, low achievers, pregnant or young parents, truant, and suspended or expelled" (p. 20). In the McCreary report, Smith et al. (2007) defined 'At risk' youth as "those youth who are marginalized, for example as a result of abuse, sexual exploitation, substance use, bullying, discrimination, mental health problems or street involvement" (p. 7) and 'high risk' youth as "the 'at risk' youth who have disconnected from school, family and community, compounding the risks and challenges in their lives" (p. 7).

I chose to include American and local definitions and descriptions from BC. Most of the literature is American, but the study is conducted in BC, Canada, therefore a local understanding must be included to bridge perceptions and beliefs.

Significance of the Study

The significance of this study is threefold. First, this study provides the unique voice and expertise of Vancouver Island alternative education administrators. Secondly, this study fills a gap in the Canadian literature regarding, alternative education, as most articles, books, and journals are American. Aside from the McCreary report (Smith, 2007), only Morrissette (2011), Nicholson and Artz (2008), Shirley (2010) and Vadeboncoeur's (2009) articles account for the relevant Canadian scholarly literature about alternative education relevant to this study. Finally, this study explores the relationship between the 21st Century Learning paradigm and alternative approaches to education. The conversation discussing this relationship is currently absent in the scholarly literature. Examining alternative education within the 21st Century Learning paradigm is significant because this concept of education reflects the principles and practices of alternative education.

Thesis Overview

This chapter introduced the topic, researcher, clientele, purpose, objectives, scope and significance of the study. Chapter two reviews the relevant literature pertaining to alternative education. Chapter three outlines the research design, epistemological assumptions, process of inquiry and ethical considerations. Chapter four answers the research questions by thematically exploring the findings that emerged from the interviews. Chapter five discusses the findings, draws a few conclusions about the efficacy and success of alternative education and ponders the relationship between the latter and 21st

Century Learning. Finally, I close the discussion with a few policy, program and practice recommendations as well as suggestions for future research endeavours.

Chapter Two: Literature Review

I uncovered very few Canadian publications, articles, government policies or reports, but found an abundance of US literature pertaining to alternative education, primarily descriptive in nature. I reviewed a number of books and selected articles from the ERIC and JSTOR databases; featuring peer-reviewed publications from JESPAR, The Clearinghouse and the Journal of Preventing School Failure: Alternative Education for Children and Youth. I also included professional publications featuring the Reclaiming Youth International organization and the American government, specifically the Office of Special Education, the Department of Education and the Urban Institute in the United States (US). This chapter is organized under the major headings of history, philosophy, purpose and typology, student profile, program features, evaluations and policy.

History

> Alternative education programs were first introduced in British Columbia in the 1960's to assist youth who were struggling in the mainstream school setting. Although the programs have evolved and changed, the overarching philosophy has remained: to assist youth to successfully attain an education in a supportive, nurturing and non-judgmental environment. Despite being around for 40 years, there has been little research published about the effectiveness of these programs in meeting the needs of the youth they serve in British Columbia. (Smith et al., 2007, p. 7)

The roots of alternative education date back to the 1960's and the Civil Rights Movement (Lange & Sletten, 2002; Smith et al., 2007; Young, 1990). Its evolution has been paralleled in Canada. In the 1960's, Free Schools and Freedom Schools gained incredible momentum and public acceptance

11

(Carswell, Hanlon, O'Grady & Watts, 2009; Gorney & Yseeldyke, 1992; Kellmayer, 1995; Kim, 2011; Kim & Taylor, 2008; McGee, 2001; Magee-Quinn, Poirier, Faller, Gable & Tonelson, 2006; Meyers, 1998; Nicholson & Artz, 2008; Raywid, 1981, 1983; Sagor, 1999; Tissington, 2006). McGee (2001) noted that "alternative schools in the 1960's and early 1970's emerged as idealistic havens" (p. 588) whereas Carswell, Hanlon, O'Grady and Watts (2009) contended that "AEPs [Alternative Education Programs] initially grew out of a desire to meet the needs of poor and minority students underserved in traditional public school systems and to create innovative programming for suburban students" (p. 446). Within this context, Aron and Zweig (2003) reflected on the tension between the initial intent of alternative education to offer something completely different and the system's need to divest itself of at-risk students from mainstream settings while retaining funding (Kim, 2011; Sagor, 2006)

In its early days, it was the *system* that was seen as unsatisfactory, *not* the students. Free Schools and Freedom Schools thrived due to heavy bank, corporate and foundation financing, "literally billions of dollars from private and government sources" (Raywid, 1981, p. 551). Raywid (1981) optimistically suggested that "the growth of the alternative school movement was further stimulated by the growing critique of education and the increasing pressures on schools to better serve each and every youngster" and saw "alternatives as a means of tailoring educational programs ... to the specific needs of different groups" (p. 553). Kellmayer (1995) commented on the difference between the discipline problems of the 1940's and 1990's, starting from chewing gum and running down the hallways to drug addiction, mental health issues, poverty and criminality. These discipline problems reflected the changes in North American society, challenging the capacity of educational systems to adapt education in public schools.

By the 1980's, the *innovative* alternative school movement had petered out. As a result, correctional and punitive programs emerged using alternative programs as 'dumping grounds' to warehouse 'outcast' students away from of mainstream schools (Dupper, 2006; Kim, 2011; Owens & Kondol, 2004; Sagor, 1999; Saunders & Saunders, 2001). During the 1980's and 1990's, alternative programs mushroomed in numbers (Aron, 2006; Aron & Zweig, 2003; Gable, Bullock & Evans, 2006; Hughes-Hassell, 2008; Kim, 2011; Kleiner, Porch & Farris, 2002; Lehr & Lange, 2003; Raywid, 1994; Saunders & Saunders, 2001; Tissington, 2006). Some school districts established alternative programs in mainstream schools and independent sites while others collaborated with community partners including community centers, correctional facilities, Aboriginal friendship centers, hospitals, rehabilitation facilities and substance abuse treatment centers (Hughes-Hassell, 2008). Lehr and Lange (2003) reflected that, in the 1980's, alternative programs primarily focused on remediation, whereas the political climate of the 1990's rekindled interest in short-term corrective and/or punitive alternative programs for disruptive students.

Recent history. In the first national survey of its kind, American researchers Kleiner, Porch and Farris (2002) reported that 39% of school districts across America operated at least one 'on-site' alternative school. When Carver and Lewis (2010) followed up on this study, they also included community-based alternative schools, reporting 64% of districts offered some form of alternative education. No equivalent report is available in Canada; hence no comparison with the United States is possible. In British Columbia (BC), the Ministry of Education drafted its first policy concerning alternative education in 2010, even though alternative programs had already existed for decades.

Philosophy, Purpose and Typology

Alternative education has lacked a clear and unifying definition as it encompassed a wide-range of philosophies, purposes and types. Lange and Sletten (2002) noted that "the constantly evolving nature of alternative programs and the rules that govern them have made them something of a moving target and difficult to describe" (p. 6). Cable, Plucker and Spradlin (2009) agreed, noting that "the philosophy and structure of one alternative school can greatly differ from the next. Ideally, alternative schools and programs are specifically tailored to support the students they are serving" (p. 3).

Philosophy. Kennedy and Morton (1999) recognized that "the anchor of the school is its philosophy" (p. 132) hence "recognizing and formalizing the philosophical position of the school... is critical to its success" (p. 125).

Vadeboncoeur (2009) believed the function of alternative schools was "to displace students who are deemed different" (p. 294), arguing that most students were usually referred to alternative schools as a last resort prior to expulsion. This Canadian researcher suggested alternative programs were "evidence of the failure of the school system, laying the blame for failure at the feet of individual youth. They highlight the inequities built into the structure of education, the inequities that necessitate alternative programs to begin with" (p. 295). This analysis echoed that of Raywid's (1981, 1983) when she questioned whose needs alternative schools were serving: Students, schools or school systems. Johnston and Wetherill (1998), Leone and Drakeford (1999), Kim and Taylor (2008) and Shirley (2010) also contributed to this discourse, questioning the underlying philosophies and purposes of alternative education throughout the decades. Magee-Quinn, Poirier, Faller, Gable and Tonelson (2006) acknowledged the philosophical tension within the field:

14

For instance, if the philosophy is that the student needs to be changed, alternative programs seek to reform the student. If the philosophy is that the system needs to be changed, the alternative program provides innovative curriculum and instructional strategies to better meet the needs of the students. This basic philosophical difference has led to decades of controversy over what the primary focus of alternative education should be and who it should educate. (p. 12)

Gable, Bullock and Evans (2006) and McNulty and Roseboro (2009) also discussed the tension between student-centered and system-driven philosophies. Van Acker (2007) believed the ideal alternative school philosophy was to "strive to provide a caring, collaborative, and engaging learning environment and to develop a community of learners that demonstrates acceptance, leadership, and academic success" (p. 6).

Purpose. There is a wide array of purposes driving alternative programs, including dropout prevention (Cable, Plucker & Spradlin, 2009; Lagana-Riordan et al., 2011; McNulty & Roseboro, 2009) remedial education (Gamble & Satcher, 2007) therapeutic restoration (D'Angelo & Zemanick, 2009; Estes 2006; Guerin & Denti, 1999), holistic development (Castaneda 1997; Oden 1995) and short term interventions (Carpenter-Aeby & Kurtz, 2000; Carswell, Hanlon, O'Grady & Watts, 2009; Nicholson & Artz, 2008).

The purpose of alternative education has been openly debated, asking whether it is meant to benefit students or the school system (Raywid, 1982; Van Acker, 2007). Most articles supported alternative programs ultimate purpose was to meet the needs of students (Aron, 2006; Aron & Zweig, 2003; Cable, Plucker & Pradlin, 2009; D'Angelo & Zemanick, 2009; De La Ossa, 2005; Dynarksi & Gleason, 2002; Gilson, 2006; Gregg, 1999; Hughes-Hassel, 2008; Kellmayer, 1995; Kennedy & Morton, 1999; Kleiner, Porch & Farris, 2002; Lagana-Riordan et al., 2011, Lange & Lehr, 1999; Lange & Sletten, 2002;

15

Meyers, 1998; Oden, 1995; Raywid 1983, 1994, 1997, 2001, 2006; Rix & Twining, 2007; Sagor, 1999; Shirley, 2010; Van Acker, 2007; Wilkins, 2008; Zweig, 2003). However, Cable, Plucker and Spradlin (2009) wisely cautioned against "generalizing advantages and disadvantages" as "alternative schools and programs differ widely in theoretical structure and purpose" (p. 2).

Meyers (1998) conducted a review of alternative schools spanning three decades. His findings presented eleven roles alternative schools could fill within the educational system, including: Vocational skill development, remedial and therapeutic environments, honing personal talents, multicultural awareness, citizenship and civic engagement, community collaboration with families and systems alike, flexible schedules, relevant curriculum and finally another educational choice supporting students and their families.

A variety of educational services have emerged in response to the diverse needs presented by the alternative education clientele (Wilkins, 2008). A combination of community, economic, educational, health and social concerns have dominated current alternative educational trends. For instance, Atkins (2008) affirmed that economics drove the existence of alternative programs while Carswell, Hanlon, O'Grady and Watts (2009) argued that current alternative schools reflected a "last chance" philosophy, as "program purposes are to 'fix the kid' and send the student back into the mainstream where they failed" (p. 448) even though this type of short-term intervention has been proven ineffective (Carpenter-Aeby & Kurtz, 2001; Cox, 1999; De la Ossa, 2005; Johnston, Cooch & Pollard, 2004; Kellmayer, 1995; McCall, 2003; Owens & Kondol, 2004; Shirley, 2010; Wolf & Wolf, 2008).

The BC Alternate Education Association (BCAEA) proposed that:

At its simplest, Alternate Education attempts to help at-risk youth, who, because of a variety of factors, are unsuccessful in the main stream. Problems experienced by these students may include a wide range of social and emotional difficulties, drug issues, trouble with the law, teenage parenthood, and a whole host of others. What these students share in common is an inability to progress satisfactorily in the regular system. In response, districts have developed a variety of models to help these students succeed. Most programs have strong links with community services, and various government ministries. Often, in addition to the teaching staff, a program will have one or more Youth Care Workers, and other liaisons with the services its students need. Programs may be small or large, attached to the main school, housed separately, or in some instances, even form their own entire high school. *The thing they all have in common is a strong desire to help kids in need, and the flexibility to tailor the programs they offer their students to best help them succeed.* (BCAEA, 2011, *emphasis added*)

Typology. Mary Ann Raywid's (1994) *Alternative Schools: The State of the Art* is the most frequently cited article about alternative education in the scholarly literature. She has researched and published dozens of articles about alternative education over the course of three decades. Raywid (1994) created a typology which has become the standard classification reference for alternative schools (Magee-Quinn, Poirier, Faller, Gable & Tonelson, 2006). A plethora of researchers have reviewed, expanded, morphed and tweaked this now classic typology (Aron, 2006; Aron & Zweig, 2003; Cable, Plucker & Spradlin, 2009; Foley & Pang, 2006; Gable, Bullock & Evans, 2006; Gilson, 2006; Gorney & Ysseldyke, 1992; Gregg, 1999; Groves, 1998; Henrich, 2005; Kim, 2011; Kleinar Porch & Farris, 2002; Lange, 1998; Lange & Sletten, 2002; Lehr & Lange, 2003; Magee-Quinn, Poirier, Faller, Gable & Tonelson, 2006; Powell, 2003; Rix & Twining, 2007; Tissington, 2006; Van Acker, 2007; Wolf & Wolf, 2008).

Raywid's (1994) typology. Briefly, Raywid (1994) classified alternative education programs into three categories: Type I (popular innovations), Type II ('last chance' programs) and Type III (remedial). Type I schools retained the pure ideals of the 1960's when innovative alternative programs sported a specific theme, were well-regarded within the educational community and truly programs of choice. Type II alternative programs were correctional and/or punitive in nature, also known as 'soft jails' that practiced behavior modification. Type III alternative programs were centred "on remedial work and on stimulating social and emotional growth" (p. 27).

Raywid (1994) realized that "alternative schools are usually identifiable as one of these three types, but particular programs can be a mix" (p. 27), depending on their clientele's needs. Other researchers acknowledged this reality (Henrich, 2005; Lange & Sletten, 2002; Powell, 2003; Van Acker, 2007), inspiring Aron and Zweig (2003), Henrich (2005) and Rix and Twinning (2009) to expand her typology even further. Kleiner, Porch and Farris (2002) credited Raywid's (1994) typology for providing a discursive framework but failed to analyze its distinctions.

Gregg (1999) produced a detailed analysis of Raywid's (1994) typology, cross-referencing each type by domains including program purpose, administration and governance, school climate, site and facilities, staffing, curriculum and instruction, entrance/exit criteria, graduation credits, special education, costs and program financing, evaluations and transportation. Aron and Zweig (2003) also reviewed Raywid's (1994) typology, arguing that Type I innovative programs were perceived as successful because students attended by choice. They asserted that Type II programs were the least successful in achieving either academic or behavioural goals because of their punitive nature and offered mixed reviews of Type III programs, proposing success hinged on students' length of stay in the programs.

18

Other typologies. Aron and Zweig (2003) expanded Raywid's (1994) typology to include a fourth type centered around students' educational needs, including those who needed a short-term bridge to return to mainstream; youth who were "prematurely transitioning to adulthood" (p.28); older students who had dropped out and now required credits for college and finally, students who were "substantially behind educationally—they have significant problems, very low reading levels, and are often way over age for grade" (p. 28) The latter was the largest and most underserviced group of them all. Aron and Zweig (2003) also considered a number of dimensions regarding program implementation, including identifying the general type of the program, target populations, focus/purpose, operational setting-proximity to K-12, location, educational focus, sponsor or administrative entity, credentials offered and funding sources.

Henrich (2005) also devised a fourth type of alternative program, however this type focussed on "promoting student self-management, using performance- based and challenging curricula, nurturing relationships, developing and providing options, being adaptive to circumstance, and retaining, establishing, or enriching integrative relationships with traditional schools so students may choose to access educational opportunities across boundaries" (p. 34). Henrich's (2005) cross-referenced dimensions by type using metaphors, intentions, foci, assumptions, aims and purposes to compare all four program types. Finally, Rix and Twining (2007) expanded Raywid's (1994) typology to include nine types of alternative program, although their analysis was not relevant to this study.

Essentially, Raywid's (1994) typology established a framework to catalogue alternative programs according to their philosophies, purposes and practices. Researchers Aron and Zweig (2003) and Henrich's (2005) expanded this original typology to include a fourth type, student-centered and

19

relationship-based, refocusing attention to the holistic needs of each student. In essence, the literature revealed a plethora of philosophies, purposes and typologies that governed alternative education, including economic, systemic and student-centered. Having reviewed the history and explored the philosophies underpinning alternative education, the next section examines the alternative student profile in greater detail within this context.

Student Profile

The consequences of students dropping out of school are costly to both the individual and society. For example, dropouts have fewer options for employment and are usually employed in low skilled, low-paying positions. Dropouts are more likely than high school graduates to experience health problems, engage in criminal activities, and become dependent on welfare and other government programs. (Martin, Tobin & Sugai, 2003, p. 10)

Estes (2006) asked: "What are troubled students?" (p. 56) Researchers consistently described at-risk students by using indicators such as academic performance, behaviour and demographic information. In BC, Smith et al. (2007) agreed with Martin, Tobin and Sugai's (2003) assessment of the risks troubled students face when they fail to graduate from high school. In the United States, Lange and Sletten (2002) discovered that alternative programs were over-represented with minority students from socio-economically lower classes. They further pondered whether students with learning disabilities would be able to retain their 'special education' services in an alternative education setting. Aron and Zweig (2003) and Tissington (2006) also used behavioural indicators, socio-economic factors and academic performance to profile students in alternative education.

In a further study, Aron (2006) specifically examined ethnicity and gender, noting that approximately 50% of Native American, black and Hispanic students graduated from high school. Girls' graduation rates were about 10% higher than boys. Van Acker (2007) also cautioned that many students in alternative programs were not designated with a learning disability or diagnosed with a behavioural disorder, thus making them ineligible for special education services.

Risk factors. A number of risk factors contributed to student school failure, including unstable housing and family dynamics, pregnancy and/or parenting, poverty and hunger, substance use and abuse, sexual exploitation, physical and emotional abuse, mental health issues and criminal involvement (Aron, 2006; Aron & Zweig, 2003; Carswell, Hanlon, O'Grady & Watts, 2009; De La Ossa, 2005; Gilson, 2006; Guerin & Denti, 1999; Johnston, Cooch & Pollard, 2004; Johnston & Wetherill, 1998; Kim & Taylor, 2008; Kleiner, Porch & Farris, 2002; Kubic Lytle & Fulkerson, 2004; Lange & Sletten, 2002; Lehr & Lange, 2003; Lehr, Tan & Ysseldyke, 2009; McGee, 2001; Nicholson & Artz, 2008; Saunders & Saunders, 2001; Smith, Gregory & Pugh, 1981; Smith et al, 2007; Tissington, 2006; Van Acker, 2007; Vanderven, 2004; Wood, 2001; Zweig, 2003).

Other frequently cited factors influencing school performance included developmental issues, learning disabilities and designations (Fuller & Sabatino, 1996; Nicholson & Artz, 2008; Platt, Case & Faessel, 2006; Wood, 2001), such as Fetal Alcohol Spectrum Disorder (FASD) (Watson, Westby & Gable, 2007), Emotional Behavioral Disorder (EBD), (Bullock & Gable, 2006; Fitzsimons-Hughes & Adera, 2006; Flower, McDaniel & Jolivette, 2011; Foley & Pang, 2006; Gorney & Ysseldyke, 1992) and Attention Deficit Hyperactivity Disorder (ADHD) (Schnoes, Reid, Wagner & Marder, 2006).

Non-academic indicators were also considered early warnings signs of possible school disengagement, substantiating Finn's (1993) contention that "dropping out of school is a cumulative process, not an impulsive action" (as cited in Martin, Tobin & Sugai, 2003, p. 11). Wood (2001) listed school-related warning signs including immature behavior or talk, hypersensitivity, irritable, tired, physical complaints, restlessness, impertinence, withdrawal, negativity and/or destructive behaviour.

Several researchers supported Wood's (2001) observations (Cable, Plucker & Spradlin, 2009; Fitzsimons-Hughes & Adera, 2006; Fuller & Sabatino, 1996; Gable, Bullock & Evans, 2006; Gilson, 2006; Lagana-Riordan et al., 2011). At-risk students were either 'pushed out' (Kelly, 1993) or eventually dropped out of school, exemplifying Cox, Davidson and Bynum's (1995) realization that "many alternative schools are dumping grounds or warehouses for social misfits and academically incompetent students" (p. 221). Several researchers supported that claim (Cable, Plucker & Spradlin, 2009; Owens & Kondol, 2004; Van Acker, 2007). McNulty and Roseboro (2009) argued that inadequately funded alternative programs fueled students' negative self-identification as 'bad kids,' impeding their attempts to succeed with the "notion that these students were unworthy of quality educational experiences, as were their more 'well-behaved' peers" (pp. 418-419).

Lehr, Tan and Ysseldyke's (2009) meta-analysis of alternative programs also identified students experiencing behavior problems without a documented disability, learning difficulties without a designation, living external stressors, social and/or emotional problems as indicators of possible school failure.

Ethnicity. American alternative programs primarily housed African-American and Latino students (Aron, 2006; Aron & Zweig, 2003; Kleiner, Porch & Farris, 2002; Lange & Sletten, 2002; Lehr & Lange, 2003; Zweig, 2003) whereas Caucasian and Aboriginal students populated alternative schools in BC with Indigenous students were over-represented in alternative programs to a ratio of 3:1 (Smith et al, 2007). Some school districts offered alternative programs exclusively for Aboriginal students. Kim and Taylor (2008) noted that alternative schools in the United States were disproportionately located in urban areas primarily populated with ethnic minorities living close to, or in poverty.

Poverty. Raywid (2001) addressed the "highly negative 'power of poverty' to predict school failure" (p. 583), echoing Payne's (1996) work on the dimensions of poverty. This contention was strongly supported in the literature (Cable, Plucker & Spradlin, 2009; Estes, 2006; Jeffries, Hollowell & Powell, 2004; Johnston, Cooch & Pollard, 2004; Nicholson & Artz, 2008; Shirley 2010). Jeffries, Hollowell and Powell (2004) and Johnston, Cooch and Pollard (2004) concluded that a student's likelihood of dropping out increased if their parent(s) had dropped out of high school too. Nicholson and Artz (2008) discovered a correlation between poverty, single parent households lead by women and school failure.

Unmet needs. Students attending alternative schools often struggled to meet their basic human needs. Gregory, Pugh and Smith (1981) contented that "alternative schools come closer to satisfying student needs, as defined by Maslow's hierarchy, than do conventional schools" (as cited in De La Ossa, 2005, p. 26). Cable, Plucker and Spradlin (2009) also realized that students were "experiencing hardships outside of school such as abuse, neglect, lack of English skills, and poor nutrition" (p. 5). Kubic, Lytle and Fulkerson (2004) quoted one administrator as saying that "the obstacles they have overcome in their general life are things that would have side-tracked my generation a hundred times over" (p. 121).

Maslow (1987) first advanced the notion that physiological needs trumped psychological, emotional, intellectual and spiritual needs. Kennedy and Morton (1999) observed that poor academic performance was automatically labelled as a student deficit and not a systemic one. Wood (2001) concurred with these observations, arguing that behaviours and poor academic output were often symptoms of greater unmet needs, such as abuse, homelessness, hunger and ill health (Smith et al., 2007). Kennedy and Morton (1999) reminded that "the purpose in listing outside stressors is to make the point that little academic learning can take place when the student is coping with multiple, major emotional stressors" (p. 56).

Disabilities and designations. Students exhibiting behavioural issues and learning disabilities were frequently referred to alternative programs (Lange & Sletten, 2002). Gorney and Ysseldyke (1992) wondered "to what extent do students with disabilities access Public Alternative Schools, Private Alternative Schools, and Area Learning Centers?" (p. 6) Lange and Sletten (2002) remarked that "the dropout rate for students with disabilities was as much as 20 percent higher than for students in the general school population" (p. 13). Furthermore, they contended that alternative schools were not designed to accommodate students with disabilities. Guerin and Denti (1999) observed that students with disabilities in alternative settings demonstrated "poor literacy and academic skills; inadequate social, emotional, and behavioral skills; alienation from school; low self-esteem; limited language proficiency; ethnic or racial discrimination; impulsivity and poor judgement, limited or unavailable adult role models" (p. 76). Gable, Bullock and Evans (2006) also argued that students with disabilities and designations were over-represented in alternative schools.

Moreover, Lehr, Tan and Ysseldyke (2009) commented on the scarcity of studies regarding students with disabilities in alternative education. Nicholson and Artz (2008) revealed that funding for 'special needs' students in BC hinged on the type and level of disability assessed. Frequently, students with mild learning disabilities did not qualify for 'special' funding, thereby

24

overpopulating alternative programs even further with a myriad of students that remained under-supported.

Alternative education literature included studies about students with designations including: Emotional/behavioral disorders (EBD), attention-deficit hyperactivity disorder (ADHD) and fetal alcohol spectrum disorder (FASD). Surprisingly, there was no literature addressing students diagnosed with autism-asperger spectrum disorder (AASD) in alternative education settings. Finally, I could not find any relevant literature addressing achievement and engagement levels for students suffering from mental health issues including anxiety, depression and other mental health issues.

Protective factors. Successful alternative programs fostered student resilience to counterbalance the risk factors impacting their lives. Successful alternative programs understood the importance of establishing a sense of belonging and welcoming atmosphere that cultivated healthy relationships where students felt respected and valued, creating a safe environment to learn. Successful alternative programs facilitated community, health and social services supports for their students beyond traditional academic programming. Gamble and Satcher (2007) believed that "programs must provide a continuum of integrated services which meet the myriad needs of this population in order to facilitate their successful re-entry into school, employment, and community" (p. 22).

Belonging. Brendtro, Brokenleg and Van Bockern (2002) suggested the most important protective factor an alternative school could provide was to foster a sense of belonging. They wrote extensively about children's need to belong through kinships, friendships, relationships, groups or support networks, as all relationships existed to meet the fundamental need to belong. Brokenleg (2005) advanced Indigenous ways of knowing as a holistic way to provide at-risk youth with a strong sense of belonging. Successful alternative schools

25

prioritized providing a welcoming environment that reached out to at-risk students. Otherwise, vulnerable youth risked falling prey to gangs and substance use issues among other pitfalls (Laursen, 2005).

Neufeld and Maté (2004) viewed belonging as a primary attachment need, discussing this concept in great detail within the context of connecting with at-risk youth. Baumeister and Leary (1995) addressed belonging from a psychological perspective, asserting that the "need to belong is a fundamental human motivation" (p. 497). They argued that "much of what human beings do is done in the service of belongingness" (p. 498), thus viewing the need to belong as purely innate. Therefore, alternative programs that created attachments with their students compensated for inadequate family and kinship relations.

Relationships and school climate. Positive and supportive student-teacher relationships were identified as *the* most important feature of an alternative program (Castaneda, 1997; De La Ossa, 2005; Fallis & Opotow, 2003; Jones, 2011; Magee-Quinn, Poirier, Faller, Gable & Tonelson, 2006; Owens & Kondol, 2004; Poyrazli et al., 2008; Raywid, 1982; San Martin & Calabrese, 2011; Wilkins, 2008; Wolf & Wolf, 2008). Zhang (2008) argued that "The heart of the success of alternative education is the teachers" and that "The importance of having dedicated, caring teachers cannot be overestimated" (p. 100).

Students identified a "warmer more friendly environment" (Raywid, 1982, p. 24) as a crucial factor that drew them in and kept them connected to their respective alternative programs (Jones, 2011; Magee-Quinn, Poirier, Faller, Gable & Tonelson, 2006; McGee, 2001; Morrissette, 2011; Owens & Kondol, 2004; San Martin & Calabrese, 2011; Wilkins, 2008). Baumeister and Leary (1995) associated overall health with belonging, noting that "social exclusion may well be the most common and important cause of anxiety" (p.

26

506) and that "considerable research shows that people who do not have adequate supportive relationships experience greater stress than those who do" (p. 508). They argued that "people who lack belongingness suffer higher levels of mental and physical illness and are relatively highly prone to a broad range of behavioral problems, ranging from traffic accidents to criminality to suicide" (p. 511). Baumeister and Leary (1995) affirmed that "abundant evidence also attests that the need to belong shapes emotion and cognition" (p. 520), supporting Native American wisdom.

Resilience. Brendtro, Brokenleg and Van Bockern (2005) claimed that "We are in the midst of a resilience revolution" (p. 134), and defined resilience as "the ability to bounce back in spite of adversity" (p. 130). Seita and Brendtro (2002) confirmed that "resilience research indicates that positive bonds to teachers and pro-social peers can off-set risk factors" (as cited in McCall, 2003, p. 115). Eheart, Power and Hopping (2003) interpreted resilience as "the ability to adapt to adverse life occurrences in a healthy way" (as cited in VanderVen, 2004, p. 96).

Larson (2005a) differentiated resilience as an internal strength and considered protective factors to be external to the person. Larson (2005b) believed youth reinforced their resilience when they could re-author their pain-filled stories from a strength-based perspective. Feinstein, Driving-Hawk and Baartman (2009) contended that:

> Native American culture provides a framework for fostering resiliency. The Lakota Sioux society identifies four core needs that foster resiliency and motivate individuals to reach their potential. These fundamental needs include belonging, mastery, independence, and generosity and are laid out in a model known as the Circle of Courage. (p. 130)

Feinstein, Driving-Hawk and Baartman (2009) provided specific strategies to help educators foster resilience in Native American adolescents, including educational and career goal setting; promoting extra-curricular activities; valuing students emotional and social needs; fostering pride and self-respect and finally incorporating Native American culture in the curriculum. Finally, Cesarone (1999) believed in the "'human capacity and ability to face, overcome, be strengthened by, and even be transformed by experiences of adversity'" (as cited in Feinstein, Driving-Hawk & Baartman, 2009, p. 12).

Alternative Programs

Raywid (1997) argued that smaller learning environments facilitated student development and engagement, maintaining that smaller schools, class sizes and student-teacher ratios were more conducive to delivering student-centered pedagogies. This section examines various models, dimensions, characteristics, features, curriculum and pedagogies associated with successful alternative schools.

Program models. Some researchers provided extensive lists of program models (Kellmayer, 1995; Lange & Sletten, 2002) while others examined program dimensions and domains (Duke & Griesdorn, 1999; Fitzsimons-Hughes & Adera, 2006). Kellmayer (1995) presented a comprehensive list of alternative education models: 1) The college-based model; 2) Schools without walls; 3) Mall/shopping district-based school; 4) Schools organized around a single unifying theme and located in an environment related to that theme; 5) Schools organized around a single unifying theme but located in an environment unrelated to that theme; 6) School within a school (full day model); 7) Schools within a school (after school model); 8) Schools located in an isolated location; 9) Elementary school model; and 10) Middle school model. Raywid (1996, 2006) and Lange and Sletten (2002) reviewed similar classification systems, identifying mini-schools and 'schools within schools' as the most common models found in alternative education.

28

In British Columbia, the McCreary report classified alternative program models according to their similarities, creating six categories: 1) day programs/day treatment programs; 2) adult graduation programs; 3) provincial resource programs; 4) community alternative education programs; 5) resource rooms/student learning centres; and 6) finally storefront programs (Smith et al., 2007).

Duke and Griesdorn (1999) and Olive (2003) examined alternative school models according to domain areas. Olive (2003) argued that at-risk students, more so than others, needed a holistic and relevant educational experience. Fitzsimons-Hughes and Adera (2006) compiled "a set of six cornerstones of effective alternative education programs" (p. 26), closely resembling Duke and Griesdorn's (1999) domains, including structural, curricular, pedagogical, staff development, administrative and evaluative areas.

Overall, most researchers agreed that offering a continuum of education services, including a wide range of alternative educational options would benefit all students (Aron, 2006; Duke & Griesdorn, 1999; Kellmayer, 1995; Kleiner, Porch & Farris, 2002; Lange & Sletten, 2002; Lehr & Lange, 2003; Raywid, 1994; Smith et al., 2007; Zweig, 2003).

Curriculum. Kellmayer (1995) believed that "affective components should be an integral part of the alternative program curriculum" (p. 31) and argued that academic achievement in effective alternative programs was based on affective, meaningful and relevant curriculum. D'Angelo and Zemanick (2009) offered four "core components of an effective curriculum" (p. 215), including a broad curricular selection; supplementary learning through complimentary computer software programs; relevant lesson plans and employing highly skilled and supportive staff. Researchers suggested that alternative programs were versatile enough to develop and facilitate meaningful curriculum (Atkins, Bullis & Todis, 2005; Fitzsimons-Hughes & Adera, 2006).

Fitzsimons-Hughes and Adera (2006) suggested that "effective alternative schools" could provide "courses relevant to students' real-world experiences that include life skills, anger management, and individual and group counseling" that reflected "an increased focus on wellness, fostering of knowledge, skills, behaviors, and attitudes necessary for social competence and adult independence" (p. 28).

Several researchers (Aron, 2006; Aron & Zweig, 2003; Kleiner, Porch & Farris, 2002; Lange & Sletten, 2002) discovered that a "disconnection between curriculum instruction and the real world as one of the primary causes of failure" (Shirley, 2010, p. 17). Phillips (1992) emphasized the importance of connecting "the related life experience of the learner; and the emotions stored in memory which relate to that learning" (p. 60).

Pedagogy. Several researchers scrutinized alternative education pedagogies (Cable, Plucker & Spradlin, 2009; Duke & Griesdorn, 1999; Dynarski & Gleason, 2002; Guerin & Denti, 1999; Hall, 2007; Johnston & Wetherill, 1998; Lange, 1998; McCall, 2003; McGee, 2001; McNulty & Roseboro, 2009; Olive, 2003; Raywid, 1982, 1994, 1996, 1997, 2001, 2006; Tobin & Sprague, 2000).

McNulty and Roseboro (2009) commented that students in alternative programs received little "beyond textbooks, which often sat unused in the classroom. Based on observations, no manipulatives, paperback trade books, science equipment, maps, or other classroom supplies that facilitate best practices were supplied. Worksheets were the primary means of instruction" (p. 419). They concluded that "the alternative school was yet another venue that failed to address many students' learning styles and educational challenges" (p. 420). Atkins, Bullis and Todis (2005) cautioned against falling back on self-paced learning and the overuse of course packs and work sheets, even if under-resourced. Conversely, many alternative programs had the flexibility to explore creative and innovative pedagogies, provided they were adequately funded, resource, staffed and supported by senior management.

Kellmayer (1995) concluded that:

Students and teachers in successful alternative programs share a sense of program ownership. Both students and teachers have considerable latitude in designing curricula, planning field trips and determining credit arrangements. Encouraged to design and implement their own vision of education and schooling, students and teachers are freed from many of the standard rules and procedures that characterize traditional programs. (p. 35).

Kellmayer (1995) also advocated for the latest technologies to support student learning. Groves (1998) found that "most of the teachers felt that what makes the program work is the flexibility that an alternative environment can offer the students" (p. 254). Kennedy and Morton (1999) strongly advocated for infusing the arts into all subjects to provide an integrated learning experience. Carpenter-Aeby and Kurtz (2001) believed in the merits of portfolio-based learning "to illustrate their experiences at the alternative school" (p. 220). Dynarski and Gleason (1999) reviewed various instructional approaches commonly found in alternative programs, including accelerated courses and project-based learning rooted in interdisciplinary practice and competency-focussed approach.

Personalized learning. Dynarski and Gleason (2002) commented that in alternative education "the range of student characteristics and needs suggests that programs designed around more individualized approaches may be better able to identify and address these diverse needs" (p. 50). Morrissette (2011) agreed that "In comparison to a regular or normal education that teaches to the mass, alternative education primarily offers students the opportunity to learn within their own style and at their own pace" (p. 170). Alternative programs have been personalizing learning for many years using many formats, creating options in response to the needs of each student, evidenced by the myriad of creative pedagogies.

Experiential and service learning. Alternative education programs have expanded their experiential learning approaches, including field trips (Johnston & Wetherill, 1998; Hall, 2007; Raywid, 1982, 1994, 1996, 1997, 2006) and service learning opportunities (Guerin & Denti, 1999; McCall, 2003; Raywid, 1982, Smith et al., 2007). Raywid (1983) included experiential and service learning components on the list of key characteristics of successful alternative programs in addition to fostering close interpersonal relationships, creating different curriculum in content and form; using descriptions to replace grades and finally ensuring a stronger individual and collective student voice. Raywid (2001) suggested student engagement depended on "'authentic' learning: unless a youngster can see value in a task and perceive it as intrinsically worth doing, he's not likely to become genuinely engaged with it" (p. 583). Smith et al. (2007) supported the assertion that volunteer opportunities and work experience were "essential components of a number of alternative education programs" (p. 48).

Vocational options. Alternative programs increasingly offered more vocational training, skill development and/or work experience opportunities (Aron, 2006; Aron & Zweig, 2003; Carswell, Hanlon, O'Grady & Watts, 2009; Foley & Pang, 2006; Kleiner, Porch & Farris, 2002; Lange & Sletten, 2002; Lehr & Lange, 2003; Long, Page, Hail, Davis & Mitchell, 2003; Platt, Casey & Faessel, 2006; Smith et al., 2007; Zweig, 2003). Aron and Zweig (2003) observed that "many alternative education programs emphasize career development or employment preparation and provide students multiple career pathway options" (p. 25).

In British Columbia, the McCreary suggested that students in alternative schools believed "more job training was needed in their community" (Smith et al., 2007, p. 26). Therefore, alternative schools that offered vocational opportunities, experiential learning and differentiated pedagogies were well positioned to support their clientele with a continuum of meaningful educational experiences and relevant training opportunities.

Integrated-community programs. Raywid (1982) emphasized that "community involvement and interaction could be extremely desirable" (p. 27) to an alternative program. Successful alternative schools provided a hub of integrated community-based support services for their students and families (Atkins, Bullis & Todis, 2005; Castaneda, 1997; Dynarski & Gleason, 2002; Foley & Pang, 2006; Kellmayer, 1995; Leone & Drakeford, 1999; Long, Page, Hail, Davis & Mitchell, 2003; McGee, 2001).

Castaneda's (1997) study highlighted the significance of community service, holistic engagement and site-level social service provision including "academic programs, personal/family counseling, drug/substance abuse counseling, peace and mediation training, medical assistance, artistic expression intervention, gang intervention, and probation services" (p. 94).) Student volunteered "in the local elementary school, senior citizens' residence and day care centers" (Castenada, 1997, p. 102). Cementing students with their community through service learning was a foundational element of this program.

Leone and Drakeford (1999) also reviewed how:

Alternative education programs need to find ways of linking their classrooms and instructional experiences to the community. Within local and regional communities are people, businesses, museums, libraries, and agencies that can provide information and learning experiences for youth. These same resources can also serve as a bridge to postsecondary

33

education or training and employment for students in the alternative school setting. (p. 87)

Kennedy and Morton (1999) suggested that "engaging volunteers is a good way to keep the community informed about the true nature of the school for healing" (p. 167). McGee (2001) and Dynarski and Gleason (2002) supported this claim. Long, Page, Hail, Davis and Mitchell (2003) believed that community health services should be based in the alternative schools, observing that students were "more willing to accept help from someone at the school than from someone at the mental health center because of the stigma associated with receiving mental health services" (p. 233).

Kleiner, Porch and Farris (2002) catalogued a list of service providers that collaborated with alternative schools, including the juvenile justice system, community mental health agencies, police and/or sheriff's department, child protection services, hospital or other health service, community organizations, family organizations, crisis intervention centers, family planning, job placement centers and local parks and recreation departments. Zweig (2003) emphasized that "connections to service providers seem critical to assist youth in overcoming their barriers to education" (p. 15), therefore:

> Recognizing the special needs of the student population in alternative schools for at-risk and vulnerable youth, many schools become service providers or facilitate services provided outside the school setting. Having youth enrolled in the alternative setting creates a genuine opportunity to reach out to the youth and address needs whether they are related to family environments, educational problems, or health issues. (Zweig, 2003, p. 17)

Atkins, Bullis and Todis (2005) and Foley and Pang (2006) also supported this position. Finally, Aron (2006) emphasized that "*reconnecting* youth requires collaboration and coordination among multiple youth serving systems" (p. 3) realizing that "no single school or program can be expected to handle such a wide array of educational and other needs" (p. 6). Overall, the literature revealed alternative schools used an array of pedagogies including experiential, personalized, service and vocational learning. Integrated-community programs were considered fundamental to the success of alternative programs and students.

Characteristics. Kellmayer (1995) listed ten key characteristics of effective alternative programs: size, location, volunteerism, participatory decision-making, curriculum, separate administrative unit, distinctive mission and family atmosphere, flexible teacher roles and program autonomy, access to social services and the use of technology.

Tobin and Sprague (2000) detailed and analyzed research-based strategies for alternative education that supported Kellmayer's (1995) characteristics including the merits of each characteristic and strategy. Lange and Sletten (2002) also identified essential elements of alternative programs including clear goals and autonomous programming (Gregg, 1999) in addition to the need for purposeful and wholehearted programming (Raywid, 1993). Lange and Sletten (2002) also voiced the benefits of praxis, arguing the need to integrate research and practice (Guerin & Denti, 1999) and link alternative schools to community services (Dynarski & Gleason, 1998; Leone & Drakeford, 1999).

Aron and Zweig (2003) reviewed a report from the National Association of State Boards of Education that identified the following elements as crucial to the success of alternative schools and students: High academic standards/expectations; high standards for interpersonal/social interactions; student-centered education and intervention plans; low teacher/student ratios; site-based management/flexibility; parent and community involvement; location and finally distinguishing between programs and schools.

Bullock (2007) characterized successful alternative schools as "student-supportive environments, with smaller classes and greater individual attention providing more opportunities for one-on-one discussions and interactions between students and teachers, and offering a more flexible and creative curriculum by providing hands-on and experiential learning opportunities" (p. 3). Wolf and Wolf (2008) identified six standards to vital to the successful delivery of alternative education services, namely:

the involvement of families, peers, schools, and communities as partners; a design that is long term, age specific, and culturally appropriate; a curriculum that teaches the application of social-emotional skills and ethical values in daily life; the inclusion of efforts to establish policies, institutional practices, and environmental supports that nurture development; the selection, training, and support of skilled staff; and engagement in evaluation and continuous improvement. (p. 190)

School climate. Several researchers cited school climate as a key element to the success of alternative programs (Aron, 2006; Aron & Zweig, 2003; Dupper, 2006; Kellmayer, 1995; Kleiner, Porch & Farris, 2002; Lange & Sletten, 2002; Lehr & Lange, 2003; Powell, 2003; Zweig, 2003). Raywid (1982) observed that the school atmosphere is likely to be "more akin to that of the family" (p. 23) reflecting "the combination of fewer regulations and increased personalization generally makes for much better student behavior" (p. 23). Kellmayer (1995) conceded that "it's much easier to foster a family atmosphere ... and promote participatory decision-making when enrollment is limited" (p. 23) and advocated the importance of embedding a student advisory system within alternative schools to actively engage students with their school plans.

The literature offered a plethora of examples that illustrated the significance of establishing a welcoming atmosphere, positive school climate and a sense of belonging (Cox, 1999; De La Ossa, 2005; Fitzsimons-Hughes &

36

Adera, 2006; Jeffries, Hollowell & Powell, 2004; Johnston, Cooch & Pollard, 2004; Jones, 2011; Kim & Taylor, 2008; Lagana-Riordan et al., 2011; Poyrazli et al., 2008; Saunders & Saunders, 2001; Wilkins, 2008). Conversely, Shirley (2010) studied an alternative school that was characterized as a 'Type II' program, struggling to engage at-risk students. Consequently, some programs did not present as "being nurturing environments for students, and does not reflect the feelings of students or parents of students who are placed in alternative schools" (p. 12).

Teacher attributes. Successful alternative education teachers held multiple roles throughout the day (Atkins, Bullis & Tobis, 2005; Jeffries, Hollowell & Powell, 2004; Kellmayer, 1995; Raywid, 1982, 1996; Saunders & Saunders, 2001). The literature abounded with desirable traits, characteristics and attributes of alternative educators. For example, good alternative educators were characterized as "caring people building a community of learners" (Gilson, 2006; p. 62) who focussed on "an awareness of the school and community resources" (Foley & Pang, 2006, p. 20). Jeffries, Hollowell and Powell (2004) highlighted "patience, persistence, courage, energy and compassion" (p. 71) while remaining "youthful, care about their students and each other, and cope with humor" (p. 73). Magee-Quinn, Poirier, Faller, Gable and Tonelson (2006) suggested that alternative educators had "more sympathetic attitudes toward their students" (p. 16). Alternative education administrators sought these traits and attributes in their staff.

From a systemic perspective, Kleiner, Porch and Farris (2002) identified a gap in tracking procedures for staffing alternative programs, noting that "there was no national data on how teachers come to teach at public alternative schools and programs" (p. 25). Research indicated that teachers were either recruited into, or chose to work in alternative schools (D'Angelo & Zemanick, 2009;

Hughes-Hassell, 2008; Kellmayer, 1995; Magee-Quinn, Poirier, Faller, Gable & Tonelson, 2006; Raywid, 1983, 1994).

Staff skills, competencies and suitability. Raywid (1982) emphasized the importance of having skilled teachers in alternative programs, describing alternative school teachers as family who are likely to provide counsel to students in addition to teaching, advising and case managing. Atkins, Bullis and Tobis (2005) commented that an educator's "ability to build relationships with students was the highest priority" (p. 268). Tissington and Grow (2007) discovered that traditional teacher preparation degrees lacked specific training to address assessment and intervention skills for teachers working with at-risk students. D'Angelo and Zemanick (2009) stated the importance of staffing alternative programs with creative and highly competent teachers who understood the necessity of building rapport with students prior to engaging in academic endeavours thus illustrating the value of "hiring staff who are flexible and willing to think outside the box" (p. 216).

Relationship-building. Kellmayer (1995) stated that alternative education settings emphasize cooperation over competition where teachers were responsible for establishing a positive climate and fostering trusting relationships with students. Jeffries, Hollowell and Powell (2004) captured the importance of allowing "a few moments of intimate conversation" (p. 76) to connect with students that was reflected by "an increased commitment to school, attachment to school, and belief in rules, along with a reduction in arrest records" (Magee-Quinn, Poirier, Faller, Gable and Tonelson, 2006, p. 15). Gable, Bullock and Evans (2006) espoused the value of trust while Johnston, Cooch and Pollard (2004) recognized the "need for a more informal, personal student/teacher relationship" (p. 28). D'Angelo and Zemanick (2009) understood that:

38

It took a substantial amount of time to build relationships with the students and convince them that the program was their key to success, which was ultimately a high school diploma. Once trust was established, the students began to see and believe that their teachers exhibited a genuine concern for their well-being that they had never seen before. (p. 216)

Atkins, Bullis and Tobis (2005) described relationships in good alternative programs as "close-knit" (p. 277). Castaneda (1997) offered examples of relationship building where "adults often sat down and ate lunch with the students, gave them rides home or rides to the bus stop, and transported the students (in their personal vehicles) to field trips" (p. 103) with a "sense of family was evidenced in many of the interactions" (p. 103). Ansell (2007) understood the dangers of disconnected youth, observing that "students who did not make a significant connection to an adult in the building were at much higher risk of not achieving graduation" (p. 10). Lange and Sletten (2002) concluded that school climate hinged on teachers' ability to establish trusting relationships with their students. Therefore, teachers who could "strengthen student connections" (p. 12) were highly valued in alternative education.

Mentorships and intergenerational relationships. Phillips (1992) remarked that "Youth often find it easier to talk with other trusted adults about sensitive but important topics than with parents" (p. 107), highlighting the power of positive relationships (Guetzloe, 1997). Struchen and Porta (1997) agreed, arguing that "students who drop out of school often cite the lack of a single person who cared about them as one of the primary reasons for leaving" (p. 119). They defined a mentor as "an older, more experienced person who seeks to further the development of character and competence in a younger person" (p. 120), elaborating on the significant role mentors play in at-risk youth's lives.

VanderVen (2004) supported this position, remarking that "the nature of the relationship developed between mentor and protégé is considered to be a more significant influence than any particular program content" (p. 97). These relationships fostered positive outcomes such as "increased resilience, improved attitude towards school and school achievement, improved problem-solving skills, higher self-esteem, better work habits, improved self-regulatory ability, and increased social skills" (p. 99). The importance of intergenerational mentorships cannot be overemphasized.

Professional development. Raywid (1993) emphasized the importance of fostering collaboration among colleagues and regularly set aside time for collective reflective practice, using both internal and external professional development opportunities. For example, Seita (2010) promoted the evidence-based Positive Peer Culture (PPC) strategy to build trust and engage at-risk youth which was based on Alfred Adler's concept of private logic combined with basic neurobiology. He emphasized the importance of building connections to create trust and provide youth with the opportunity to build healthy relationships. Seita (2010) maintained that all behaviour was a form of communication that should not be taken personally, recognizing that adults needed to "skillfully and intentionally hear the voices of young people as a source of empowerment and a window into their private logic" (p. 51). The four principles of Positive Peer Culture included not taking what the youth say and do personally; listening and seeking to decode what is actually being said; being alert to learning opportunities; and creating a culture of belonging. Similarly, Reed (2011) supported Urie Bronfenbrenner's ecological view of the child, advocating that "every child needs at least one person who is irrationally crazy about him or her" (p. 53).

In addition to basic skills and competencies, alternative teachers must be capable of developing trusting relationships with students, foster intergenerational mentorships, develop meaningful curriculum, and deliver innovative programs that accommodate a myriad of learning modalities including experiential, vocational and service learning. Furthermore, alternative teachers were expected to maintain current and relevant professional development training.

Assessments and intervention strategies. Dynarski and Gleason (2002) recommended that "rather than thinking about which program should be created as an intervention, it may be more useful for educators and policymakers to develop intervention strategies" (pp. 44-45) specific to individual students. Platt, Casey and Faessel (2006) agreed, proposing that students were better served by holistic assessments than generic program interventions. Interventions strategies such as Individual Education Plans (IEP) and Individual Instruction Plans (IIP) were designed based on numerous academic, behavioural and psycho-educational assessments. Smith et al. (2007) remarked that in BC, "All youth in alternative education programs are entitled to have an IEP" (p. 42) which is "a written plan developed for a youth, which describes the services, program modifications and/or adaptations that are to be provided" (p. 42). Individualizing student plans and personalizing educational programs reflected decades of successful practice in the alternative education field.

Entrance and exit criteria. Raywid (1982, 2001) questioned if students had any voice students in referral to an alternative school. Kleiner, Porch and Farris (2002) catalogued a comprehensive list of entrance criteria for alternative schools that was based on criminal offenses or school rule breaches, including possession and/or distribution of drugs and alcohol, involvement in physical altercations, severe truancy, weapon use and/or possession, progressive academic failure, disruptive behaviour, firearm use and/or possession, criminal involvement, pregnancy, parenthood and mental health needs. They reported that over one third of school districts considered "involvement with the juvenile justice system as a sufficient reason for transfer to an alternative school" (p. 17).

Reasons such as "history of social-emotional problems, truancy problems" (Foley & Pang, 2006, p. 15) were sufficient to be referred to an alternative program. Leone and Drakeford (1999) astutely observed that "failure in traditional middle school and high school programs was a prerequisite for admission" (p. 86) to alternative schools. In the 1990's, Castleberry and Enger (1998) cited "disruptive behavior" (p. 105) as the most frequently cited reason for referral to alternative schools. Atkins (2008) emphasized that academic or behavioural difficulties were precursors to initiating referrals to alternative schools, contending that current alternative programs were "driven more by school districts' desire to prevent a loss of revenue due to students 'dropping out' than for the good of students" (p. 346).

Lange and Lehr (1999) presented alternative education as a viable choice for at-risk students. Lehr, Tan and Ysseldyke (2009) studied entrance criteria for alternative schools and discovered four general criteria: "meeting some form of at-risk criteria, being suspended or expelled from a regular school, being disruptive in the general education environment, and not achieving success in a traditional school setting" (p. 26). Cable, Plucker and Spradlin (2009) supported these findings, identifying "poor grades, chronic truancy, disruptive behavior such as fighting and other maladaptive behavior, including drug or alcohol use and/or arrests that lead to suspension or expulsion...family crisis, prolonged illness, and social or emotional issues" (p. 4). Carpenter-Aeby and Kurtz (2001) described a unique program where referrals hinged on their full time social worker's assessment.

Entrance and exit criteria varied according to students' personal circumstances, program model and availability. Smith et al. (2007) reported that most alternative programs operated on a year-long "continuous intake process"

42

(p. 38) while concurrently maintaining waiting lists. Kleiner, Porch and Farris (2002) listed commonly cited exit criteria for alternative programs as improved attitude and/or behaviour, student motivated to return to their school, improved grades, administrative approval at the alternative and mainstream school, student deemed ready by standardized measures and availability of space. However, they only addressed short-term criteria, not long-term student learning plans. Research suggested that students needed to be disruptive to be referred to an alternative program and stable to be referred back to mainstream.

Flexible attendance policies. Epp and Epp (2001) identified rigid attendance and program practices as counter-intuitive to school engagement, arguing that undue strictness could permanently "drive students from the school system" (p. 240). For at-risk students, "it is better to start at 10 a.m. than not at all" (p. 240) as "alternative schools encourage students who may not be early risers" (p. 241) to maintain a connection to their school community. Lange and Sletten (2002) shared student feedback praising the merits of flexibility in alternative education, championing the significance of having "choice and flexibility as central to their decisions to attend the alternative programs and in their persistence at the programs" (p. 17).

Furthermore, Jeffries, Hollowell and Powell (2004) reported student feedback that "relaxed attendance policies" (p. 75) were seen as one of alternative education's greatest features. Smith et al. (2007) echoed that flexible attendance policies were "vital for those experiencing chaotic home lives, mental health or addiction issues, or returning to education after a lengthy absence" and that it kept "youth connected, as 30% reported that the flexibility was a factor that kept them attending their program" (p. 40).

Funding. Jeffries, Hollowell and Powell (2004) warned that smaller alternative schools were frequently at risk of losing their funding and being shut down. Atkins, Bullis and Todis (2005) supported these findings, noting that "inadequate funding was overwhelmingly cited (95%) as being a barrier for the success of alternative education programs" (p. 255). Alternative programs in the United States commonly accessed philanthropic foundations for funding (Raywid, 1996). Alternative programs in British Columbia frequently competed for grants to supplement their core funding. For example, Nicholson and Artz (2008) remarked that the Ministry for Children and Family Development (MCFD) in British Columbia was a crucial source of funding for alternative programs, via grants promoting specific projects and objectives. They remarked that funding for alternative programs was more accessible in the 1980's. Aron and Zweig (2003) commented that:

> Most alternative education programs' budgets are based on a variety of unreliable funding sources, such as grants, charitable contributions, and fees for service. Some alternative education programs may also receive state and local education funds—although these funds are often less than the per-pupil funding that traditional schools receive (NGA Center, 2001). (p. 30)

Aron (2006) identified state funding as the primary source, "followed by local funds, grants or private contracts" (p. 21), emphasizing "The challenges of tapping into these funding streams should not be underestimated. Navigating local school district financing is a complex task" (p. 22). Furthermore, Foley and Pang (2006) remarked that "accessibility to libraries and science laboratories appears to be more limited" (p. 14) and that too often "alternative schools fail to seek or receive their fair share of revenues budgeted for students' education when compared to the expenditures per pupil in traditional schools" (p. 16-17).

Facilities and site location. Alternative schools were located in a variety of settings, including independent sites, classrooms in large high schools and portables on mainstream campuses. Kellmayer (1995) reviewed the advantages

44

and disadvantages of each, suggesting independent sites minimized stigma while other researchers argued that on-site facilities allowed all students to share school grounds and facilities for extra-curricular activities. There have been no evaluations directly comparing the efficacy or success of each model.

Kleiner, Porch and Farris (2002) revealed that 59% of alternative schools were housed in separate facilities while some programs were housed in regular schools during and after school, others were located in community and recreation centers, former school buildings, juvenile correctional facilities and detention centers, store-front in neighbourhood organizations, public housing projects, shelters, health facilities including substance use treatment centers and post-secondary campuses. Foley and Pang (2006) reported that "a majority of the principals of alternative education programs" (p. 17) preferred separate facilities. However, quite often, these facilities were "often 'hand-me-down' buildings" that did not "meet the physical needs of an innovative educational program" (p. 17). Van Acker (2007) validated these findings by stating that "these programs often lack the adequate facilities, materials, and budgets necessary for success" (p. 7). Even though alternative school location influenced attendance and school engagement, this issue was not adequately addressed in the literature.

Evaluations

McGee (2001) advocated that alternative schools should make a point of documenting their success. Lange and Sletten (2002) remarked that "the larger question for many in the alternative school movement is whether the desired outcomes for these students can be focused narrowly on academic outcomes or whether a broader measure of effectiveness is needed." (p. 22). Researchers in alternative education often argued against alternative programs being subject to the same criteria as mainstream schools (Lange & Lehr, 1999; Lehr & Lange,

2003; Lehr, Tan & Ysseldyke, 2009; Nicholson & Artz, 2008; Oden, 1995). Alternative education advocates argued that their programs served a vastly different clientele, specifically, students that were rejected from the mainstream system. Oden (1995) argued that "as a consequence of the predominance of outcomes-oriented program evaluations, educational researchers found they had an insufficient understanding of the content and processes of the approaches or programs they studied in classrooms or schools" (p. 177). Lehr, Tan and Ysseldyke (2009) contented that it was paramount for alternative schools to document their successes to continue to secure funding to service at-risk students. They suggested that "Progress indicators in areas beyond academic performance may be necessary to capture the impact of alternative schools on student outcomes" (p. 30).

Nicholson and Artz (2008) critiqued the Ministry of Education for basing success exclusively on the results of standardized testing, arguing that alternative programs required more holistic evaluation criteria to represent their work. American researchers also supported this position (Lange & Lehr, 1999; Lehr & Lange, 2003; Lehr, Tan & Ysseldyke, 2009; McGee, 2001, Van Acker, 2007; Wolf & Wolf, 2008). McGee (2001) suggested that continuous evaluation and "opportunity for real world practice of social skills, conflict resolution, anger management, and problem solving techniques" (p. 27) were essential to student success. Van Acker (2007) suggested that "Empirically validated prevention and intervention strategies that target developmental risk factors show the greatest impact" (p. 8). Lehr and Lange (2003) reminded that:

> Because many alternative schools focus on promoting youth development and education across many domains (e.g., social, academic, emotional, vocational), measuring academic progress alone may not capture the richness of what some alternative schools offer and the changes that can occur for youth who attend. (p. 63)

46

Failed return to mainstream. Kellmayer (1995) recognized that "Many alternative programs operate under the erroneous assumption that after a certain period of time in the program, students will want to return to a traditional program" (p. 27). Owens and Kondol (2004) agreed as did De la Ossa (2005). Aron and Zweig (2003) pondered this tension as well, debating whether or not it was in the students' best interest to transition back to a mainstream school.

Students were customarily referred to alternative programs with the ultimate goal of reintegrating them back into mainstream classes. However studies revealed student regression occurred when returned to a mainstream setting (Aron & Zweig, 2003; Cox, 1999; McCall, 2003; Wolf & Wolf, 2008). Cox (1999) and McCall (2003) questioned this practice, arguing that the positive effects of alternative education were short-lived and dissolved when students returned to mainstream.

Wolf and Wolf (2008) observed that students experienced improvements in alternative schools because they were "provided with social services, small classes, and counseling" (p. 211). The positive effects of being in an alternative setting dissipated over time. Consequently, Wolf and Wolf (2008) argued that "alternative school programs...ought to provide 'long-term care'" (p. 211) in lieu of short term interventions. Kellmayer (1995) agreed, providing a comprehensive evaluation checklist for alternative schools that included measures beyond traditional academic performance and attendance.

BC Ministry of Education Policy

Atkins, Bullis and Todis (2005) suggested that sound alternative education policies attracted and retained students to their programs. These included "(a) flexible attendance options (b) smoking policies (c) school completion options, and (d) a 'no expulsion' policy" (p. 273). Epp and Epp (2001) suggested mainstream schools used policies to exclude difficult students.

47

Kellmayer (1995) recommended that alternative schools have "a separate administrative unit" (p. 32), as they provided a different service to a different clientele.

Alternative education policy. The BC Ministry of Education established its first Alternative Education policy in 2010, legitimizing alternative education within the overall educational system, defining:

Alternate education school programs – Type 3 facilities – focus on the educational, social and emotional issues for those students whose needs are not being met in a traditional school program. An alternate education program provides its support through differentiated instruction, program delivery and enhanced counselling services based on student need. (BC Min. of Ed, 2010b)

The policy's rationale acknowledged that:

Students who attend alternate education school programs are most often the most vulnerable population in the school system. Alternate education school programs have disproportionate numbers of children and youth in care, Aboriginal students, children and youth living in poverty or the street, gifted children who have difficulty in social situations, children and youth involved in drugs, alcohol and the sex trade and youth with mental health concerns. Alternate education programs offer an opportunity for these vulnerable and at-risk students to experience success. (BC Min. of Ed., 2010b)

Over time, alternative schools have narrowed their focus, specifically offering educational services to at-risk youth (Kelly, 1993). School completion rates remained low in BC, particularly in districts heavily populated by Aboriginal students, other ethnic minorities and low-income families (BC Min.of Ed., 2012). Recently, a BC Ministry of Education report indicated graduation rates ranged from 70-80% province-wide; with approximately 50%

48

of Aboriginal students completing high school between 2005 and 2010. (BC Min. of Ed., 2012).

21st Century Learning. In *A Vision for 21st Century Education*, The Premier's Technology Council (2010) stated that BC needed to shift how it thought about and delivered public education, using relevant technologies to remain globally competitive "regardless of socio-economic background" (p. 1). This vision document argued that, in education, 'one size does not fit all.' Students will progressively "engage with their own content, at their own pace of learning and take an increasing role in charting a path best suited to those talents, interests and abilities" requiring "a more project-based or problem-based approach" (p. 2) to engage and interest students in their learning. Simultaneously, the BC Ministry of Education advanced their 21st Century Learning paradigm, advocating for a new way to engage learners:

> Personalized learning for each student in British Columbia means a shift from a set of broad, uniform learning outcomes and courses, to learning that is increasingly student-initiated and self directed. It is learning that is co-planned with students, parents, and teachers. (BC Min. of Ed, 2010a)

Chapter Summary

This literature review examined the history, philosophy and purpose of alternative education, crystallizing in Raywid's (1994) typology as the foundational classification system in the field. This review detailed risk factors impacting the lives of alternative students, including demographics such as ethnicity, poverty and unmet basic needs in addition to examining the implications of academic designations and learning disabilities. Resilience, a sense of belonging, positive school relationships and a welcoming climate were identified as protective factors counteracting risk factors and other impediments to school success.

Several alternative program features were reviewed including program domains, dimensions and models, curriculum and pedagogy including experiential, personalized, service and vocational learning in addition to community-integrated programming. The literature review illustrated key program characteristics such as school climate, assessment and intervention strategies in addition to staff attributes primarily featuring relationships-building skills. Administrative considerations were scrutinized, focussing on entrance and exit criteria, flexible attendance policies, funding sources, site and facilities considerations. The paucity of meaningful evaluations and appropriate criteria were briefly discussed, closing the chapter with a look at BC's alternative education policy and a few government publications elucidating the 21st Century Learning paradigm.

Chapter three addresses the research design, defining specific methodological terms, detailing research components including participant selection, data collection, organization, analysis and qualitative validation. Finally, ethical considerations are reviewed, as are the delimitations and limitations of the study.

Chapter Three: Methodology

I conducted this study using a qualitative research design, defined by Creswell (1998) as "an inquiry process of understanding based on distinct methodological traditions of inquiry that explore a social or human problem. The researcher builds a complex, holistic picture, analyzes words, reports detailed views of informants, and conducts the study in a natural setting" (p. 15). This view was reiterated by a myriad of qualitative researcher experts (Creswell, 1998, 2003; Crotty, 1998; Denzin & Lincoln, 1994, 2000, 2005; Denzin, Lincoln & Smith, 2008; Fine, Weis, Weseen & Wong, 2000; Guba & Lincoln, 2005; Janesick, 2000; Mertens, 2005; Patton, 2002; Richardson & St-Pierre, 2005; Sandberg, 2005; Shank, 1994). I based the research on an Interpretivist epistemology (Crotty, 1998; Heidegger, 1982; Holdstein & Gubrium, 2005; Kvale, 1983; Miles & Huberman, 1994; Moustakas, 1994; Schwandt, 2002) that followed phenomenological principles (Crotty 1998; Giorgi, 1985).

Denzin and Lincoln (2000) emphasized that qualitative research "does not belong to a single discipline", nor does it privilege one "methodological practice over another" (p. 6). Crotty (1998) argued that interpretivism "emerged in contradistinction to positivism in attempts to understand and explain human and social reality" (pp. 66-67). Unlike a quantitative study grounded in a scientifically neutral positivist approach, Crotty (1998) maintained that "The Interpretivist approach, to the contrary, looks for culturally derived and historically situated interpretation of the social-life world" (p. 67). I chose a phenomenological approach to truly understand (*verteshen*) the purpose and values governing alternative education by exploring the lived experiences and perspectives of its administrators. Giorgi (1985) viewed phenomenology as going "to the everyday world where people are living through various phenomena in actual situations" (p. 8). I provided thick and rich descriptions of participants' experiences and explored alternative education's relevance within both the general context of education and the recently proposed 21st Century personalized learning paradigm.

In this chapter, I provide relevant methodological definitions and discuss pertinent epistemological considerations that underpin this qualitative study. I also share the reasoning behind my process of inquiry and detail my research methods, participant selection strategy, and data collection process. I address the rationale supporting the organization, processing and analysis of the data. Finally, I review ethical considerations and procedures that framed this study and provide the reasoning that guided the methodological authenticity, credibility and trustworthiness of this research design.

Definition of Terms

This section contains relevant methodological definitions to contextualize my position and provide scope to the study.

Epistemology is "the theory of knowledge embedded in the theoretical perspective and thereby in the methodology" (Crotty, 1998, p. 3). It encapsulates *"how we know what we know"* (p. 8, *emphasis in original*). According to Hamlyn (1995), epistemology deals with "the nature of knowledge, its possibility, scope and general basis" (as cited in Crotty, 1998, p. 8).

Interpretivism, a theoretical perspective within the constructionist worldview, is defined as "overwhelmingly oriented towards an uncritical exploration of cultural meaning" (Crotty, 1998, p. 60) where "most interpretivists today embrace such accounts as descriptions of authentic 'lived experience'" (p. 159).

After having reviewed the seminal works of established qualitative researchers discussing their divergent interpretations of phenomenology, Giorgi (1985) concluded that a "consensual, unequivocal interpretation of phenomenology is hard to find" (pp. 23-24). Overall, he suggested "to be phenomenological, in general, means to return to the phenomena themselves, to obtain a description of those phenomena, to submit them to imaginative variation, and then obtain an eidetic intuition of their structures" (p. 26). In so doing, the qualitative researcher seeks "substance significance" (Patton, 2002, p. 467) and not quantitative statistical significance when establishing the validity (authenticity), reliability (credibility) and rigor (trustworthiness) of his or her research. In the phenomenological tradition, the researcher seeks *verstehen* (to understand): "to what extent and in what ways do the findings increase and deepen understanding of the phenomenon studied" (p. 467), hence to genuinely understand the participants 'lived experienced' from their unique point of view. According to the phenomenological tradition, researchers must "bracket" (i.e. *epoche*), their personal views and biases to remain open to participants' lived experiences and refrain from viewing from one's perspective.

Creswell (1998) addressed the concept of analytical bracketing (*epoche*) by borrowing Moustakas' (1994) understanding of transcendental phenomenology, which initially emerged through the work of Husserl. He maintained that researchers were required to set aside their preconceptions when studying any phenomenon. Patton (2002) agreed, remarking that "in taking on the perspective of *epoche*, the researcher looks inside to become aware of personal bias, to eliminate personal involvement with the subject material, that is, eliminate, or at least gain clarity about, preconceptions" (p. 485).

Patton (2002) advanced that "the logic of criterion sampling is to review and study all cases that meet some predetermined criterion of importance, a strategy common in quality assurance efforts" (p. 238). He qualified purposeful sampling as "the logic and power of purposeful sampling lie in selecting information-rich cases for study in-depth" (p. 230) and purposeful random sampling as "not a representative random sample. The purpose of a small sample is credibility, not representativeness. A random sample aims to reduce suspicion about why certain cases were selected for study" (p. 241). Finally, he described key informants as "people who are particularly knowledgeable about the inquiry setting and articulate about their knowledge" (p. 321)

Methodology: Qualitative Research Design

I chose an interpretivist epistemology based on Crotty's (1998) classification system for qualitative approaches to social research. I wanted to grasp the participants' lived experiences and understand their perspectives regarding alternative education. The aim of interpretivism is to accurately understand participants' lived experiences by providing thick and rich descriptions as part of a comprehensive approach to qualitative data analysis. Consequently, I connected concepts and themes repeatedly found in alternative education literature to the practical wisdom and professional experience of the participants.

In keeping with the phenomenological tradition, I remained vigilant and keenly aware of the importance of respecting the principles of "analytical bracketing" (Kvale, 1996, p. 54) during and after the interview process (Creswell, 1998; Lichtman, 2010; Moustakas, 1994). Grounding myself in the practice of *epoche* (Sandberg, 2005), I suspended my perspectives (Heidegger, 1982; Holstein & Gubrium, 2005) to the best of my ability during both the data collection and analysis process. As Sandberg (2005) remarked, "the aim of *epoche* is to ensure that the researcher withholds his or her theories and prejudices when interpreting lived experience" (p. 60). I was curious to

54

understand (*verstehen*) the alternative education system, its students and its place on the continuum of educational services.

Schwandt (2000) cautioned that "phenomenology means something far more complicated than a romanticized notion of seeing the world of actors 'as it really is'" (p. 206). I appreciated that "knowledge of what others are doing and saying always depends upon some background or context of other meanings, beliefs, values, practices and so forth" (p. 201). For this reason, I remained particularly aware of the importance of maintaining the integrity of the data collection, organization and analysis process.

To ensure a phenomenological mindset, I imagined Shank and Villella's (2004) lantern metaphor: "lanterns are used to allow light to illuminate dark areas so that we can see things that previously were obscure" (p. 48). This phenomenological metaphor advanced the notion that new data are not discovered, but revealed once illuminated. Therefore, my "lantern" consisted of semi-structured interviews with three alternative education administrators. Each participant was invited to share their experiences, feelings, thoughts and reflections regarding all things alternative education. Additionally, I polled eleven delegates from the annual alternative education conference. I conducted 'one question' random interviews to represent alternative educators' opinions from across BC.

The following section details my specific research methods and participant selection process, including sampling strategy and recruitment approach. I addressed ethical issues including the study's limitations. Finally, I provided the details involved in my data collection, organization and analysis process.

Specific Methods

For the purposes of this study, I selected semi-structured interviews to collect the data. Kvale (1996) described the research interview as "an interview whose purpose is to obtain description of the life world of the interviewee with respect to interpreting the meaning of the described phenomena" (pp. 5-6). Shank (2006) argued that "it is almost impossible to do good qualitative research without learning how to interview someone" (p. 38). The interview questions I designed were congruent with Kvale's (1996) conception of the research interview and can be found in Appendix A. I prepared myself to conduct these interviews by investigating the principles and practices of conducting research interviews within the qualitative research paradigm, including the importance of maintaining awareness, integrity and professionalism. Fontana and Frey (2005) emphasized that:

> The new empathic approaches take an ethical stance in favour of the individual or group being studied. The interviewer becomes an advocate and partner in the study, hoping to be able to use the results to advocate social policies and ameliorate the conditions of the interviewee. The preference is to study oppressed and underdeveloped groups. (p. 696)

With nearly two decades of relationship-building experience working with and interviewing marginalized youth and families, I felt confident proceeding with this research design. Although I was conscious to minimize the impact of my biases by bracketing my views, I was personally aware of my supportive predisposition towards alternative education.

I held all three semi-structured interviews in the administrators' offices. The interviews ranged in duration from sixty to ninety minutes each. I used a digital audio recorder to record the interviews. I transcribed each interview according to a predetermined transcription guide and returned each transcript to the participants for their verification. Upon completion of the member-check

56

and approval from the participants, I proceeded to organize and analyze the data.

I decided to keep a research journal to document my thoughts and feelings about the interviews, my reflections about the research process and engage in 'stream of consciousness' writing to allow any unexpressed and/or subdued thoughts to emerge. I documented my observations about the data and reactions to it, thereby enriching the qualitative validity (authenticity, credibility, trustworthiness) of the research instrument (me).

Participant Selection: Sampling and Recruitment

Sampling strategy. I began with a criterion sampling strategy described by Patton (2002) to ensure I selected school districts with alternative education programs, schools or departments. Within that sample, I selected "key informants" (Patton, 2002, p. 321) who were in a position to provide the richest data possible. Patton (2002) stated that "purposeful sampling focused on selecting information-rich cases whose study will illuminate the questions under study" (p. 230), remaining consistent with this research design and criterion sampling principles. My units of analysis consisted of individual participants to capture "what is happening to individuals in a setting and how individuals are affected by the setting" (Patton, 2002, p. 228). For the purposes of this study, I interviewed three alternative school administrators within the central Vancouver Island region.

Recruitment approach. Prior to engaging in interviews, I required approval from the University of Victoria's Human Research Ethics Board (see Appendix B), to meet "the ethical standards required by Canadian universities and national regulatory bodies" (HREB, 2010). Upon approval, I contacted three central Vancouver Island school districts to request permission to conduct research (see Appendix C) and was directed to connect with each alternative education principal. Fortunately, all three principals agreed to an interview. I provided them with all relevant documentation pertaining to the research and interview process, including an abstract, information letters and consent forms (Appendices D & E). Sessions were booked shortly thereafter upon mutual agreement.

Data Collection, Organization and Analysis

Data collection. I provided each participant with the interview questions in advance to give them the opportunity to process and reflect, thereby allowing me to collect thoughtful, accurate and relevant data. During the interviews, I noticed that one of the participants had written notes by the questions while the others responded more spontaneously. I used a semi-structured interview format to allow room for digression, diverging somewhat from the topic while still ensuring that all of my questions were thoroughly addressed. I realized that participants often responded to questions before they were asked, digressing, no matter how much flow I designed into the interview questions.

I ensured that I could return to previous questions for clarity and/or further details while maintaining a conversational atmosphere within the semi-structured interview format. I made certain that all major topics were addressed, including: the participants' interpretation of alternative education; their educational, vocational and professional development backgrounds; abilities, skills, knowledge, attributes and character traits sought in staff or possessing themselves to work in this field. I reviewed indicators used to measure success of alternative students and factors identified with effective alternative programs. Finally, I invited participants to comment on any links they perceived between the proposed 21st Century personalized learning paradigm and alternative education philosophies and practices.

Technologically, I became more adept with the digital recorder from one interview to the next, learning its features, where to position the microphone for best sound quality, being more aware of background noises. For example, a tree service (cutting, pruning and shredding) began operating directly outside the window where first interview was taking place. In the second interview, a spoon rattled on the table next to the recorder. By the thirst interview, I was hyper-vigilant about placing the recorder away from possible background noises.

Data organization. I used the *N'Vivo 10* qualitative software application to process my transcripts. This computer program facilitated the research process by expediting coding and queries, allowing greater accuracy and depth of analysis. I was able to identify themes and streamline the analytic process by using the *N-Vivo* software program. I first used an open coding process (Patton, 2002), coding each interview independently to ensure that I allowed themes to emerge naturally. Some themes I anticipated while others I did not. I then cross-coded each transcript by coding each question across all of the transcripts to ensure I had not neglected or misinterpreted data. Once I completed three rounds of coding, a number of themes emerged allowing me to sort, organize and collate data bits efficiently. The program functions allowed me to run queries, create graphs and build matrices to flesh out the particulars of any given theme, much more efficiently than manually. As Bazeley (2007) suggested, *N'Vivo 10* provided the built-in versatility to examine data in greater depth, building and reworking themes within each topic area. The software program included features such as word frequency and framework matrices, saving me countless hours of collecting, organizing and sorting data into meaningful themes.

Data analysis. Prein, Bird and Kelle (1995) cautioned researchers about thinking that software *did* the analysis for them, as its function was to facilitate and expedite traditional data analysis methods. The coding process allowed me to revisit participant responses numerous times, often coding data into multiple categories. This approach enabled an intricate analysis, shedding light on the depth and nuances of the data. (Weitzman, 2000) As the themes emerged, it became nearly impossible to contain data within one classification. Several coded passages could be classified into more than one category, occasionally creating more confusion than clarity.

For example, data could be used to answer more than one research question, including definitions of alternative education; formal education, vocational training and professional development; identifying successful program features, creative programming and pedagogical practices. Finally, the same data could also be used to clarify the relationship between the 21st Century personalized learning paradigm and alternative education. As with the data collection process, phenomenological principles and values governed the analytic process, thereby safeguarding the data from my personal preconceptions.

Delimitations and Limitations

Delimitations. I provided as rich an understanding of alternative education, its scope and clientele as possible by limiting the number of participants to three and defining a specific geographic area. I selected key informants, namely three administrators, from alternative schools in the central Vancouver Island region because of their extensive experience within the public school system, all starting as teachers and counsellors prior to becoming administrators.

Limitations. The primary limitation of this study is the inability to replicate it. This research endeavour is qualitative in nature, relying on the experiences, interpretations and perceptions of the participants that are specific to them and their geographic location. A further limitation was the absence of a

60

national database collating educational data across Canada, preventing an international comparison between American and Canadian data. Education falls under provincial jurisdiction in Canada. The final limitation was the complete lack of available female participants for this study. All administrators were male.

Authenticity, Credibility and Trustworthiness

Obtaining authentic, credible and trustworthy data was vital to the integrity of this qualitative study (Creswell 1998, Mertens 2005, Patton 2002). I adopted Richardson and St-Pierre's (2005) concept of crystal refraction to respect the "multidimensionality" of perspectives found in sound qualitative research. Richardson and St-Pierre (2005) maintained that knowing "what we see depends on our angle of repose" (p. 963). This point underscored the importance of realizing that there are no untainted objective truths to be discovered, but a variety of interpretations depending on our perspectives, worldviews and beliefs.

Consequently, the authenticity, credibility and trustworthiness of qualitative findings were enhanced when data was examined from as many angles as possible. Richardson and St-Pierre (2005) provided valuable insights into the world of qualitative data analysis. Their crystalline analogy substantiated the integrity of a rich qualitative research design. I extracted the essence from each respondent's interview by using a multilayered coding process, also revealing students', parents', school boards' and trustees' perspectives in addition to community and public perceptions regarding alternative education programs.

Guba and Lincoln (2005) suggested that an ethical relationship, in and of itself, was a form of qualitative validity. They presented seven standards they believe strengthen the core of qualitative data, including positionality, specific discourse communities, voice, reflexivity, reciprocity, sacredness and perquisites of academic standing. I remained aware of these seven standards, understanding the importance of keeping the integrity of the study intact.

Creswell and Miller (2010) suggested a number of validity checks appropriate to qualitative research paradigms. For example, I enhanced the authenticity, credibility and trustworthiness of the study by adopting a reflexive stance, keeping a journal and engaging collaboratively with participants. I built in a debriefing process with close peers and colleagues to ensure that I maintained an appropriately balanced perspective throughout the research process. I followed a "member-checking" protocol by providing participants with their transcripts, asking them to review and approve the documents before I proceeded any further. This promoted "verisimilitude" (p. 129) between the interview and transcript.

I also incorporated Shank's (1994) notion of 'abductive reasoning" where "clues are held together, not by theory, but by their phenomenological relationship to each other" (p. 353). By "leaving [my] own suppositions of expertise behind and dealing with the actual experiences and impressions of the experts participants" (Shank, 1994, p. 355), I upheld the phenomenological tradition to the best of my ability, bracketing my views and suspending my beliefs.

Kvale (1994) argued that "the focus on the interviewer as an instrument puts strong demands on the empathy and competency of the interviewer" (p. 159). Fontana and Frey (2000) suggested that establishing rapport and trust with the participants were crucial components to maintaining the authenticity of the data. Genuine interest, rapport and trust cannot be feigned but were developed through the researcher's sincerity and ability to authentically connect with their participants. Fortunately, I have embedded these competencies, skills and abilities throughout my career, enabling me to engage participants in empathetic, respectful and caring manner.

Therefore, the data's authenticity was maintained through genuine interactions with the participants, credibility was upheld by cross-referencing all coding multiple times and finally trustworthiness was embedded by selecting ethically grounded participants. I used Richardson and St-Pierre's (2005) crystalline scheme to validate my qualitative data. Finally, by remaining self-aware and transparent about my own views and biases, I maintained the distinction between fact, opinion and interpretation to the best of my ability.

Ethical Considerations

I meticulously followed all informed consent procedures and confidentiality protocols approved by The University of Victoria's Human Research Ethics Board (HREB). I advised participants of their right to withdraw their participation and data at any time without explanation. I compensated each participant with a $10 Starbucks gift card at the end of the interview, thanking them for their time and engagement. I treated all participants with respect, ensuring they understood the purpose of the study and the expectations regarding their participation. All participants received a copy of their interview transcript for review. One participant also requested and received a copy of the recording itself.

There is a slight risk that the participants' confidentiality might be compromised. There are only four school districts within the central Vancouver Island region, three of which are represented in this study. Every effort was made to conceal the identity of each participant by changing their names, omitting locations and avoiding the publication of identifiable details which could reveal their or their school district's identity. However, given the small size and uniqueness of some of the alternative programs, people with local knowledge could identify the participants and their locations.

In the consent form, each participant was asked to agree for me to keep the data indefinitely, should I pursue doctoral studies, publish an article or present the findings at academic or professional conference. I also discussed this with the participants prior to their signing the form. All electronic data was secured, password protected and securely backed up on a secondary password-protected drive. All physical data, notes and files have been locked away in a secure cabinet, as per the ethics board requirements.

Summary

This chapter presented my detailed research design. I identified my epistemological and theoretical stances in addition to detailing my methodology, featuring the semi-structured interview as my specific research method. I explained the rationale underlying my participant selection process, sampling strategy and recruitment approach. I addressed my data collection process, data organization approach and data analysis procedures. I discussed issues regarding qualitative research validity, i.e.: Authenticity, credibility and trustworthiness. Finally, I examined relevant ethical considerations and concerns, including the limitations of the study. The next chapter answers the initial research questions and the final chapter discusses the findings, shared conclusions and offers recommendations for further research and practice, all for the purpose of enhancing alternative education services in British Columbia.

Chapter Four: Findings

The purpose of this study was to explore successful alternative schools, program models and practices in central Vancouver Island. After much deliberation and reflection, I distilled my focus into the following research questions:

1) How is alternative education defined, described and understood, in contrast to mainstream public education?

2) How does one measure student success and evaluate program efficacy in alternative schools?

3) What existing approaches and/or theoretical models make alternative education viable within the 21st Century learning paradigm?

Simply, I wanted to know what alternative education was, who it was meant for and why it existed. I wanted to know how it worked and how we knew it was actually effective. I was curious if current alternative programs were congruent with the 21st Century Learning paradigm. My responses to these questions were based on the data I collected from three interviews with alternative education principals. In short, I learned that alternative education is a legitimate pathway to graduation, or school completion, for students who were not successful in the mainstream educational system.

Introducing the Participants

I interviewed three alternative education principals from the central Vancouver Island region. These men combined for a total of 85 years of experience in public education, as teachers, counsellors and principals. John and Terry claimed 34 years of experience each, while Leo had been in the education field for 17 years at the time of these interviews. They also combined for 63 years of experience in alternative education and 47 years as administrators. John and Leo spent the majority of their careers in alternative education while Terry joined alternative education after initially spending 19 years in the mainstream school system.

John provided a glimpse of his personal and professional background, shedding light on his interest in alternative education:

Maybe growing up in East Vancouver and always being on the edge (chuckle) and having my share of troubles in high school, absolutely, yeah, probably those things. And I was exposed too in Richmond, I did a lot of T.O.C.'ing in alternate and that kind of environment really appealed to me.

Leo recalled being recruited at the time by the alternative education principal:

When I was T.O.C.'ing, the first year I was out of university, I was T.O.C.'ing and I got into to ... inner schools ... probably one of the toughest schools we've got in our district, and I happen to get a long stint there teaching a music class and everybody was worried at the school that I wouldn't be able to do it but I had them, no problem, captivated the entire time I was there. So the secretary there was the wife of the principal here. He called me, literally, as soon as I was done down there, saying "Can you come up here and try some T.O.C.'ing up here?" And I did and it worked out well and then he just gave me a job the next year ... and I think that's kind of how it happens in alt. ed., is you get noticed as having, maybe not great teaching, like I'm not a fantastic science teacher, I'm not a fantastic English teacher, but I've just, I'm really good with the kids and that's what I look for in my teachers here, teachers who really connect well with the kids.

Terry voiced his personal inclination and professional philosophy that

66

drew him to alternative education:

> For me, ... first off, there's a philosophical premise ... I always had an
> inclination to find ways to make education successful for *all* students,
> both when I was a teacher, certainly when I was a counsellor, I mean that
> was who I worked with a large part, because that's why they were coming
> to counselling, and ... thirdly, as a principal ... These are kids who are
> 'alternate' kids ... So, the district ... had somewhat of an idea that we
> needed to move in different directions ... and that my career had largely
> been devoted to finding ways to meet the needs of all students. So ... we
> talked about perhaps me taking over the alternative programs ... I made it
> clear that if the district gave me the support, that he would see some
> great- miraculous changes in the next few years. So that was a pretty
> exciting challenge to be given and 1997-1998 was my first year, and I'm
> very proud, 15 years later, to say that we exceeded, I think, any
> expectations that I had, or the district had to moving down that vision.

Terry decided to retire at the end of the school year because "one of my
visions in my retirement ... after 34 years in the school district to move on to
other work; one of which will be consulting work, and another will be possible
work at the university level." All three participants engaged in the alternative
education field purposefully, with a passion and desire to serve students the
mainstream system was unable to support. Consequently, I selected these
participants specifically because of their expertise and experience working in a
marginalized and often completely unrecognized educational field.

Understanding Alternative Education

The first research question asked: How is alternative education defined,
described and understood, in contrast to mainstream public education?
Participants responded by referencing philosophies, purposes and theories,

client profiles and Ministry of Education policy. They critiqued the mainstream school system for its inability to meet to the needs of all students, thereby triaging at-risk students to alternative programs.

A student-centered approach characterized alternative education philosophies, theories and purposes. One participant used analogies and metaphors to illustrate the connection between philosophy, theory, purpose and practice. 'At-risk' students were characterized using external descriptors such as socio-economic risk factors and school-based designations. Alternative programs were juxtaposed against mainstream schools, revealing a negative stigma attached to the word 'alternative.' Policy governing alternative education in BC was presented to conclude the findings.

Alternative education philosophies. Participants advanced that child-centered educational philosophies were the cornerstones of successful alternative programs. Terry related the importance of connecting educational philosophy directly to practice. Over the course of the interview, he referenced the Starfish analogy and Ameba metaphor several times to illustrate what student-centered philosophies look like in action. For a greater understanding of the Starfish story, please see Figure 1 below.

Starfish analogy.

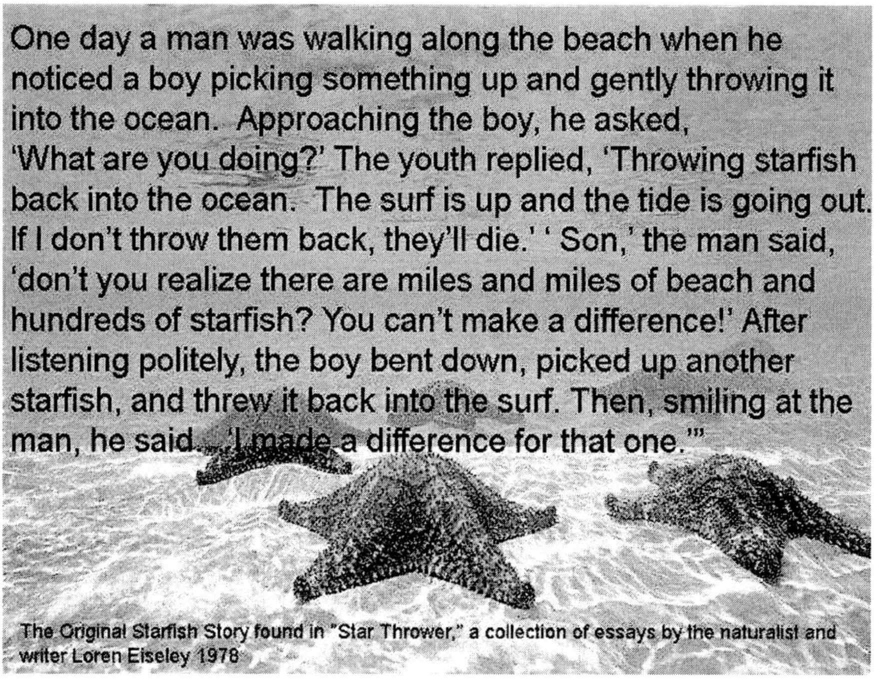

One day a man was walking along the beach when he noticed a boy picking something up and gently throwing it into the ocean. Approaching the boy, he asked, 'What are you doing?' The youth replied, 'Throwing starfish back into the ocean. The surf is up and the tide is going out. If I don't throw them back, they'll die.' ' Son,' the man said, 'don't you realize there are miles and miles of beach and hundreds of starfish? You can't make a difference!' After listening politely, the boy bent down, picked up another starfish, and threw it back into the surf. Then, smiling at the man, he said...'I made a difference for that one.'"

The Original Starfish Story found in "Star Thrower," a collection of essays by the naturalist and writer Loren Eiseley 1978

Figure 1: **Starfish analogy (Lesley's Coffee Spot, 2012, retrieved from Google images)**

Terry reflected on the Starfish analogy:

each one of those starfish, each one of those individual students ... have personal talents, assets, skills and needs and we need to analyze each of those and ... create a learning plan that is truly that student's learning plan, not a template from somebody else ... that's philosophically what we're all about here ... our success is driven one student at a time. It's driven by an overall vision of where we need to go to meet the greatest needs but its practical implementation is one student at a time.

Ameba metaphor. Terry illustrated alternative education's flexibility by referencing the ameba metaphor. He believed education was a "service industry" where "the needs of the student need to drive the system, not the needs of the system driving the needs of the student." Terry believed a flexible system was better suited to engage students and customize their learning plans according to their interests, needs and talents. He cautioned against alternative schools replicating the rigid structures of mainstream schools:

That alternate program is ... different, but if it also has those rigid boundaries, if the walls ... are the walls of that regular school, then what happens when the students don't fit that? Where do they go? So, what we recognized early on ... is that we ... needed to be like an ameba, and there's my metaphor. It needed to be something that would shape to its environment or that whatever came into it would shape the ameba. And recognizing that, when student A comes in, the ameba needs to bend here; when student B comes in, the ameba needs to bend there. And it needs to be constantly; it's this living organism that has to adjust to the clients that it has, not just the clients it envisioned it would have but the clients who truly come in the door... To be that ameba ... and to be able to mold and shift ... on a monthly basis and a daily basis but hour to hour. Where are we at today and what's happening and what's going on in my community, what's going on for our students and 'how can we adjust today?' always being in concert with a larger vision. So it's looking at the macro and channelling it down to the micro. 'What am I doing this very minute with that student?'

For Terry, the ameba metaphor meant deliberately being "on the edge of chaos:"

That has to be right front and center. We have to be able to do that ... I mean you can have total flexibility, which is basically anarchy and then there's nothing happening and there's no system to what you're trying to do, there's no process, there's few goals, it's like hit and miss, etc. So, you have to be very deliberate on the edge of chaos. You have to be very systematic on the edge of chaos. But you have to be able to be flexible as you move through that maze.

The modern-day village. Terry also reiterated the old proverb "it takes a whole village to raise a child." In alternative schools, that village consisted of teams of people that coordinated their efforts to meet the needs of their students. He spoke of collaboration with local service providers, community partners and stakeholders to access resources. Staff forged alliances within the community to recreate that modern-day village: "we understand that we can't do it by ourselves, working in very non-traditional type situations." Wrap-around services were commonly initiated and facilitated by alternative school personnel in this study.

Terry spoke at greatest length about alternative education's student-centered philosophy using the Starfish, ameba and village analogies to richly illustrate these fundamental beliefs underpinning student-centered alternative education philosophy.

Theories into Practice

Leo heralded Ruby Payne's work on generational poverty, Gordon Neufeld's research on attachment theory and Abraham Maslow's theory detailing the hierarchy of needs. These developmental and humanistic theories drew attention to the importance of meeting the physiological and psychological needs of students first. Leo also referenced Martin Brokenleg's work on Indigenous ways of reclaiming at-risk youth, a meaningful approach in the central Vancouver Island region.

Terry believed the role of alternative schools was to help at-risk youth meet their basic needs, reclaiming and restoring to move forward with their schooling, vocational training and employment readiness. Sometimes this meant addressing housing and hunger needs, creating trust and supporting the student until they were ready to move on. He maintained that taking the time and attention to address these needs was an essential first step before students could learn. Terry firmly believed that it was the responsibility of the alternative schools to respond to the needs of their students. He espoused Maslow's hierarchy of needs in practice (see Figure 2). For example:

> if one of those clients comes in, and where they're at is, they do not have the physiological needs of their life being met, they don't have enough food and water, and we're here trying to, as the school system is, self-actualize them, make them the best they can be; there's this huge gap between the reality and the vision of where we'd like them to go... So, the whole understanding of the needs of our students ... was based on what I would call the lower levels ... of Maslow's hierarchy around the physiological needs, around the needs for safety, around the needs for connectedness and belonging.

Figure 2: Maslow's hierarchy of needs (Dreamstime, 2012, retrieved from Google images)

Terry illustrated what working according to Maslow's hierarchy of needs looked like on a daily basis:

What has been the curriculum for Johnny? Well, the curriculum for Johnny was first off, we got him in the door; secondly, we started to help him meet some of the lower levels of Maslow's hierarchy, we got him connected with housing, we found, maybe initially, we got him off the street into a transition house, or the hostel or some place. We eventually work with the Ministry of Children and Families ... and got him into a foster home, or we got him independent living or whatever it was. And then we worked with his mental health worker because Johnny has some huge issues and we drove him to appointments and we worked with him here and we got him into some of our small groups, etc. And the advisor is all the time building, we're always building relationship and all of a sudden after, maybe for Johnny that would have taken weeks that might have taken months, it might even sometimes take years. That's what I call the first stages of what we got to do, but we got to do it, *cuz if we don't do that, Johnny's gone*. We're no good to Johnny if we are not willing to take that time.

Purpose of Alternative Education

Participants unanimously agreed that the purpose of alternative education was to meet the needs of students by providing them with alternative pathways to graduation or school completion. Their programs did so by first meeting the physiological and psychological needs of their students and then went on to engage them with their schooling. Terry championed the principles, educational and humanistic purposes of alternative programs:

We're the alternative programs. We exist to meet the needs of those students who aren't functioning in that other environment, that need the

74

time for us to build those relationships, heal the wounds do what is necessary to get them to the stage where they can start moving forward.

Introducing the Students

Students attending alternative schools were profiled using risk factors and school designations. Participants shared vignettes that exemplified the common barriers and challenges faced by many of their students. Terry described his clientele as "the underdog... the less advantaged, the marginalized, the vulnerable within our system." He believed that "the school system has notoriously, sometimes not done a good job with disadvantaged students ... the ones who didn't fit the system." Terry explained that his students "come to us disenchanted, disengaged, disenfranchised and damaged," reflecting the typical profile of alternative school students.

Risk factors. John shared the following characterization to illustrate how an at-risk student might experience school:

'how the fuck can you relate to my crazy world?' where 'yeah, I don't understand fractions 'cuz ... my alcoholic dad was beating the shit out of my mom all night long. And then when I went to school the next day I didn't get fractions.' You know, how do you relate to it?

John's vignette exemplified the lived experiences many of his students faced during their adolescent years. Matters involving unstable housing, volatile family dynamics, and mental health and addiction issues frequently permeated students' lives, particularly those from lower socio-economic levels.

Poverty. Participants voiced their awareness regarding socio-economic barriers and associated issues in addition to dealing with the inflexible, and sometimes confusing, mainstream school system. Leo discussed the impact of generational poverty at great length, including collateral issues including volatile family dynamics, housing instability, and mental health and addictions.

He recommended the work of Ruby Payne for people working in alternative education settings:

A lot of our kids are locked into generational poverty. Their parents lived in poverty; their parents' parents lived in poverty, so that's all they know. And part of living in poverty has nothing to do with graduation ... So breaking that cycle, helping them break out of that cycle of poverty is very difficult. But for us, if we can help them break out of that cycle of 'education isn't important'... Breaking out of that ... 'My parents made it on welfare; I can make it on welfare.'

Poverty-related issues impeded students' ability to concentrate on schoolwork and successfully navigate the mainstream educational system, particularly for First Nations students. He remarked that one of his literacy programs was mostly comprised of Aboriginal students, further accentuating the correlation between poverty and Canada's Indigenous people. Furthermore, Leo addressed the challenges experienced by his independent living students:

Right now, we've probably got, I'd say I think 10 kids that are living independently. We've got at least a handful of kids that don't have a place to live. They couch surf and that's just their world. So we deal with a lot of troubles, a lot of issues ... [they need]
a warm place where they can have some food and socially interact.... 'Guess what? Johnny didn't sleep anywhere warm last night. He was in Tim Horton's all night.' And, Maslow, right? ... They just need that, a nice safe environment for a few years... If a kid is hungry, we take care of him. We got a full lunch program here and a hot food, or hot breakfast program too. So any kid, who the kids I said are living on their own, or the kids who are couch surfing, it's free; kids who are in poverty, it's free. Other kids, we just charge them a buck, doesn't cost very much. It's a cheap good meal ... we're very fortunate to have that 'community links'

money. That would be horrible if we ever lost that. That would just kill us.

Terry also needed to remind his staff that although it would be easier:

to have our students come from good homes, from healthy environments, well adjusted, no mental health issues, with good literacy and numeracy skills, proper nutrition, etc., etc., etc.... But the reality is, the reason our students need an alternative is they don't have those things.

He selected staff that understood the dimensions of poverty and could relate to the students:

traditionally those people who go into education as teachers and others, we've generally come from white Anglo-Saxon middle class backgrounds. And, yet, we're not dealing with students who come from those environments. So if we don't understand poverty, if we don't understand all the dimensions of poverty and what- how does that affect how you view the world and how you function and certainly one of our professional development pieces was for a number of years to look at the work of Ruby Payne and a number of other people who had done some remarkable work around the dimensions of poverty and the culture of poverty. We need to constantly do that and we need to constantly challenge our own our own belief sets.

Leo also observed mental health issues including anxiety and depression interfered with students' ability to focus and learn. He ascertained that about 95% of his student body smoked marijuana, half of them claiming habitual use. For example, during an intake meeting, Leo shared that a prospective student argued that cannabis grew brain cells. He gave other examples illustrating the impact of mental health and addictions issues, particularly on students from lower socio-economic levels. Leo shared many stories including examples of students struggling with suicidal ideation, mental health and addiction issues.

Student designations. Academic, behavioural and/or health related 'designations' identifying learning disabilities, behavioural disorders and other health-related deficits were common to students in alternative schools. John's alternative school offered an early intervention program for younger students designated with "most severe behaviours." This program integrated "kids that are predisposed to come to our ... program, which is 9 seats for 11 and 12 year-olds, 'cause they're just gonna turn the middle schools upside-down' and we know that, why do that?" John believed that if we "support them now, give them a good flavour for this place and then when we ... bring them into our, our 8:30 'til noon, Monday through Friday ... school", they would be familiar with the school and staff. These younger 'designated' students "need a lot of support" and may not "have the wherewithal to be in a classroom with 15, 16 other kids and ... not going to be destroying that classroom."

Theoretically, the purpose of assigning designations to students was to identify deficits and find ways to accommodate and support these students. When mainstream schools found themselves unable to adequately support these 'designated' students, they referred them to alternative programs. John understood these students to be "our really most damaged kids and neediest kids for sure. They don't have the wherewithal to be in a classroom and not destroy it, so they're out there in the shop and doing various things." Their "various designations ... don't fit any one categ- they don't fit G or K or D or H ... they're interspersed ... they're designated one way but they could ... have 3 or 4 types of designations."

Terry designed his programs to have the ability to respond to the wide-ranging abilities, capacities, learning styles and needs each student presented. If a student was:

such a kinesthetic learner, we need to have hands-on opportunities for them. We need to have things that are out in the community and that's a big piece of where we're going with trying to meet the needs of our students who are cognitively challenged and have many of those, many that are fitting the K category, less than a 70 IQ, etc. Students who are FASD, who intellectually have certain talents etc., but there's huge gaps, there's huge pieces missing that will never be repaired, unfortunately. So how do we ... build their resilience and their coping? How do we work with them? How do we deal with the students [whose] ... adaptive skills are extremely challenged, or their executive functioning skills are extremely challenged? We've identified, actually in our programs, 50 to 70 of our students fit those types of descriptions.

This study's findings revealed poverty-related risk factors including volatile family dynamics, housing instability, and mental health and addiction issues impacting their ability to function in school. Furthermore, although school-based 'designations' identified the need for adaptive pedagogy or extra supports, the mainstream educational system struggled to meet these needs. Poverty-related barriers and learning challenges impeded students' ability to learn and function in mainstream and Alternative schools.

Systemic Failures

Alternative programs would be unnecessary if mainstream schools were equipped to meet the needs of all students. Leo suggested misplaced transition points between schools fueled student attrition by being positioned at developmentally awkward times in a student's K-12 career. He noted that his referrals were sourced from catchments with multiple transition points:

I think that's really hard on kids, especially our Aboriginal population. Our Aboriginal population in town here they go K to 6, in elementary school, then they get up and move again in grade 7 to our middle schools which are more junior high-ish than middle, 7 and 9. And then, by grade

8, grade 9, they're getting settled there and guess what, we're going to pick you up and now move you in grade 10 to the high school. So not only is the move to a new school challenging enough, they're moving into a new school in the most important and toughest year of their K to 12 life: Grade 10. And what happens is, a lot of them last a semester, maybe a semester and a half and then they drop out... And then we try our best to get them caught up and back on track. So transition points, out of all of the schools ... in the district that feed students to me, the school I get the fewest referrals for is the school in the in the part of the community that only has one transition point. They do K to 7 ... and 8 to 12... So there's only one transition point, and the transition point isn't grade 10, it's not grade 9, it's grade 8. You got 2 years to settle with the school, get to know the staff and it's small, it's not 1100 kids, it's only 370 or 360 or something. You get to know all the staff and get to know all the students ... So I get fewer referrals from there than any other schools.

Leo also critiqued mainstream schools in particular for having rigid structures embedded in rotating block schedules as contributing factors to student failure:

We've got... big challenges with that in our district. Because in our district, we've got 4 different high schools with 4 different grading models, on 4 different timetables. So, we don't even have the ability for kids to move between schools to take 'you know, I really want to be part of this program at that school for this block' there's no flexibility for that, none, not in our district right now. We've been talking about it for years but there's still a bit of a reluctance to move to that... It's really, it's hard. And I say that, our system here is pretty easy: I have 5 periods a day. Your period one never changes, your period two never changes, period three never changes. And I still get kids in the office here: 'where am I

80

supposed to be right now?' And they've been here for months. So how the heck can they figure it out down there? It's near impossible.

Leo levelled another critique against the Ministry of Education for making the new 2004 graduation plan more difficult to achieve:

P.E. was never part of the program, and then in addition to that, 4 mandatory provincial exams at the grade 10-11 level. Science 10, English 10, Math 10 and Socials 11 which has become a huge barrier and that's where a lot of our kids end up falling by the waste side at the high schools. They fall out in grade 10. They do grade 10 once, they don't pass, they try again they still don't pass. They come to me... and it's the toughest year. If they can get through grade 10 at a high school, they'll most often make it to graduation, unless there's a huge bump in their personal world. But, the reality is for a lot of them they can't, it's hard... The other big challenge we see is in the numeracy world. We used to assess every kid that came in here in their math. We do just an easy assessment now. But when we did the full assessment, probably about 98 percent of the kids that came here were between 2 and 3 and 4 grade levels below in math... So they would come in, usually around a grade, between grade 4 and grade 5 math levels. Occasionally maybe one or two kids a year, they would actually come right at grade level. Most of them are below. So that's a huge challenge cuz this new math curriculum they came out with ... it's killing our kids right now because, two sides: One is a lot of our literacy kids, we can sometimes get them to a point where they can be successful in Communications 11 and 12, meeting the reading writing component of the graduation. But the challenging part is that the math is so text-based and so multilevel, that these kids are going into the program, and I've had kids in math 10 now for a year and a half

81

and are still only in the beginning units. They just can't ... It takes all day just to do a few questions.

According to these findings, poorly placed transition points, structural rigidity and more rigorous academic graduation standards contributed to student attrition from mainstream schools.

Stigma. Students, staff and programs were also subjected to negative stigma by working at or attending alternative schools. Alternative schools were used as dumping grounds for difficult students and staff. For these reasons, when Terry accepted the alternative education principalship, he demanded the full support of his superiors:

at that time, the alternate programs ... were very much like the traditional alternate programs around the province; they were somewhat ghettoized ...'Well, we're going to find that old building and we're going to that's- we're going to give a couple of teachers and keep those kids out of the regular school system and warehouse them' so to speak. That's perhaps a little bit too blunt ... but I know that is the model that happens all across North America in alternate education.

Terry emphasized that:

kids who are in alternative programs are not second class citizens and again that was one of the things that we said, I said early on with our school district is I don't want to be a part of something that ghettoizes kids.

He critiqued school districts for fueling the negative stigma attached to alternative programs by using them as dumping grounds for nearly retired employees:

Unfortunately ... it was also a place that somebody who was ready to retire could be shuffled off into something that was, in the eyes of a school district, 'well that's less demanding because those kids never go to

82

school anyways' and so we're going to put Mr Jones or Mr Bill or Mr Fred over there. And, I think any of us who pretended that that didn't happen we're hiding our heads in the sand.

John chose to address stigma in alternative education from a different perspective. Although mainstream schools referred students to alternative schools with the "caveat" that they "can quote-unquote 'fix the kid' and put them back in the middle school," John iterated that "we'll do it, but we don't, we're certainly not gonna reward a student that is successful here by putting them back to everything that was unacceptable about their lives before this ... their unhappy place before this, right?" John's welcomed the stigma as he saw it as an opportunity to inform people about the merits of alternative education:

It's not like when I started here in 1988 and I had 5 kids and I was out in this old schoolhouse building that's since been demolished ... when a parent came to me bawling their eyes out because 'I was told that in alternate schools the kids smoke dope with the teachers' and she had worked herself into a complete lather over that issue ... but it's not quite that bad, but there still is always a stigma attached, which I love, I hope it never goes away. I absolutely love it cuz it's a beautiful opportunity for me to educate ignorant people.

The word 'alternative' school had an inherent negative connotation, being interpreted as 'less than' instead of 'equal but different', its actual meaning. Participants knew their alternative schools were being used as 'dumping grounds' for problematic staff and students. They also realized how educators, students and programs were stigmatized. Each of them addressed the 'stigmatization' issue in their own unique ways.

Provincial Policy

In 2010, the BC Ministry of Education tabled its inaugural policy on alternative education. All three participants contributed to its development. The Ministry of Education alternative education representative realized that BC had no policy governing alternative education. Once in place, this policy legitimized and validated the existence of alternative education as an important contributor to the public education system. John recalled that:

> it was her initiative to get us in the same room, to get Island administrators... in a restaurant in Victoria, about 6 of us and ... we hammered it out. And we took a couple of weeks ... but it... wasn't neglect, that's my point ... It was more like an employee with the Ministry of Education ... who's been in Alternate Ed. and in Adult Ed. forever and her heart is exactly there saying 'Oh my God, I need to insulate Alternate Education in the province by good policy and we don't have it folks, so let's build it.' That's the way it came about.

Leo informed that this new policy required "every alternate program has to have an intake process" and a personalized learning plan for each student to deter mainstream schools from using alternative schools as dumping grounds for at-risk students. Terry remarked feeling "very fortunate to be part of a group of alternate ed. administrators... to actually help them create – what had never been in place – was an alternate ed. policy." As a result, this policy has:

> some of the audit criteria that's now in place. What is Type 3 alternate program that's going to be funded full time for a student taking only one course? Well, you have to have all these other things in place that we're talking about here today. If you're not doing that, then you're warehousing and you shouldn't be funded fully. But that's what we have to look at is creating those best practices.

Participants heralded the advent of this new alternative education policy as it acknowledged their existence for the first time. They felt alternative education was now legitimized by having a policy that ensured each student had a personalized plan.

Understanding Alternative Education Summary

The first research question asked: How is alternative education defined, described and understood, in contrast to mainstream public education? It is defined according to student-centered philosophies and theories that support alternative education's fundamental purpose: to meet the real needs of their students. Terry articulated the Starfish analogy, Ameba metaphor and village allegory to illustrate how these philosophies support students. Maslow's hierarchy of needs was highly touted as the primary theory espoused to support at-risk students. Leo further referenced Neufeld's attachment theory and Brokenleg's Indigenous approach to reclaiming at-risk youth. Both Leo and Terry championed Payne's work on generational poverty as fundamental to understanding their clientele.

Participants shared their backgrounds, profiled students according to risk factors and school designations. They critiqued mainstream schools, the educational system and the Ministry of Education for failing to meet the needs of all students. They reflected on alternative schools reputation for being dumping grounds for troublesome staff and students, inevitably drawing a negative stigma. Finally, recent policy was discussed as a huge leap forward to protect alternative education and advance best practices in BC.

Therefore, how is alternative education defined, described and understood, in contrast to mainstream public education? It can be defined as a legitimate pathway to high school graduation or school completion. It can be described as student-centered philosophies, purposefully remaining flexible to meet the needs of their students. Alternative schools understood the need to prioritize meeting basic needs first, prior to endeavouring into learning. Our participants heralded alternative programs as modern-day villages that facilitated access to community-based resources and services for students and their families.

Evaluating Alternative Education

The second research question broadly asked: How does one measure student success and evaluate program efficacy in alternative schools? Measuring student success and evaluating program efficacy was contingent upon factors including supportive leadership, advocacy, funding and staffing considerations in addition to school climate, and relationships with staff, student engagement and supportive community alliances. Indicators including accredited graduation plans, successful transitions to post-secondary institutions and the work force were also noted. Most importantly, participants suggested that relevant benchmarks and appropriate targets be used to assess success and efficacy.

Leadership Responsibilities

Participants identified funding constraints and staffing challenges as issues inherent to administering alternative programs. Continuous advocacy on behalf of their students, staff and programs was said to be the most effective approach to addressing such challenges.

Advocacy. Advocacy was identified as one of the most important functions of an alternative school administrator. For example, Terry and John believed in sheltering staff from board politics, advocating for resources and forging community partnerships as primary leadership responsibilities. John remarked that:

> if you don't have a supportive board and if you don't have a supportive
> district admin you will create it by your success, and that's the way we've

86

always operated.... And if you don't have support from district admin or school trustees are new, you build support by being successful in the community ... And yes when they first came in did I go to them with a list of randomly chosen kids, of about 12 kids and told their anonymous stories to those trustees and ... they never got over it? ... How damaged those kids were and their resilience and their sense of humour etc., and what they've accomplished given ... what they came to us with.... So, there's that we wanted trustees to hear. And here we are, our first exposure, alternate ed., to our new trustees and the buzz in the room is the buzz that was carried from the foyer because Teddy (student) was in the foyer and there were about 12 middle school kids who were coming to present right after Teddy and I on their science projects, but just before they went in the room, they all started this chatter "it's Teddy, it's Teddy, Teddy from Hornby", right (laughter) he was like a God for them. And so we were swept in right to the board to do our presentation based on these little middle school kids being so dramatically impacted by this successful alternate school kid.

Terry reflected that:

my job as an administrator, as a leader, a principal in this program is to be that buffer between the work we need to do in this program and the realities of, sometimes what a school district faces and what the Ministry faces and kind of be that point... that is absolutely the role of the principal and leaders in an environment like this because there has to be, again, that buffer between the work that we're doing on a daily basis and the system, cuz the system is the system and when superintendents are being told by the Ministry 'thou shalt do this and we're not happy that you're not doing enough of that' that all trickles down to the to the system and so if you're the renegade out there saying 'screw you' to the system, you're not probably going to be very effective because you're going to undermine yourself ... but, you do have to be strong-willed and you do have to be willing to do battle, but you also have to understand that it's not their fault that they don't understand. And rather than just getting angry, you have ... educate trustees educate district staff, and work within- and even Ministry staff, to help them understand that the needs are different...

Terry recollected:

I had a battle once with one of our district staff who said "Terry, you don't have enough urgency over graduation." And to put it bluntly, and you can edit whatever, I said 'Fuck you! We have the most urgency about graduation, but we understand there's a process to that. We understand that unless we do these other things, we don't have a hope in hell of getting Johnny to that point. So, if you want to just have him become another statistic, or you want to say Johnny no longer counts and we're only going to take kids who are ready then now you're talking about the regular system' ... We need people who can be leaders for all students, not just certain types of students.

Funding. Unstable funding sources impeded the ability of alternative programs to provide adequate educational services. Budgetary shortfalls manifested themselves as outdated and irrelevant educational resources, under-staffed and ill-staffed programs and scarce professional development opportunities. John shared how the combination of funding cuts and reduced grant availability prevented him from staffing his support positions fulltime or providing reasonable transportation for his students. Terry recognized how funding was "a finite pot." As a result, his team "utilized all of our school-based days; we utilized every grant that we would be able to get, we utilized finding ways to have staff doing work in the summer time, we worked with other alternate programs" to beef up the educational services they could provide.

Leo expressed his frustration with the current funding structure that undercut his students. He advocated that funding should be targeted and follow the students who generated it to support individual students and the alternative programs that actually provide personalized educational services. However, 'designation' funding was lumped into general revenue and redistributed at the board's discretion. Administrators became forced to apply for additional grants to adequately run their schools. For example, Leo applied for and received a "reclaiming at-risk youth" grant to "recapture kids that hadn't been engaged in school." He shared that:

> I've been harping on this for years; they got to target the funding. The reality is that in many districts, they use alternate ed. as a cash cow. They stuff the kids in, under support them, and then take that money and funnel it off to other programs, which to me, seems completely backwards because these are the most needy kids in our district. And really, if our, one of the goals, which I know it is in many districts and in the province is to increase graduation rates, what population do we need to target? You don't need to help out the 70% that are graduating, let's help out the 20% who are not and come walking in here. It's all these kids and in every district, it's the alternate kids that need that extra support and... It doesn't follow the kids. And I've been pushing our district to move toward more of a model like that [site-based funding]. But ... I do get support there... We're still not, I don't think, doing enough, here. We're still losing kids, we shouldn't lose anybody. Why? Why would we lose a kid? We shouldn't, we can get them in the door; we should be able to keep them.

Leo referred me to a nearby school district that successfully used a site-based funding model to support their alternative programs. He reiterated that if school districts were funded to support students with designations, the money should follow them. Funding inequities were affecting the ability of alternative programs to reasonably support their students. Leo's message was clear: "Target, target, target! Target the funding!"

School Climate. A crucial factor affecting student engagement in alternative education settings was having whether their program provided a safe and supportive environment. Leo believed that establishing respectful environments fueled by healthy relationships significantly influenced student success:

> We do get some of the toughest kids in the district here. The kids they cannot handle the regular system. That's why they're here. And they've all got baggage and they've all got issues, but if you create that environment where they feel safe and respected and valued, they'll do the stuff called 'school work' and eventually graduate. And sometimes it's not even for them; they want to do it with their families, or even for us. It's like 'Leo, I know, I'll get it done, I'll get it done!'

Having a "caring atmosphere is huge" and knowing that "our kids want to be here" were clear indicators of program efficacy. Leo understood that the importance of providing his clientele with a safe place where they belonged:

> For many of our kids, I've talked about some homeless kids that we've got, or kids who live independently, have very little connection with any family. This is their family, right? ... a couple of years ago, I had a group of kids, it was the end of Christmas break and we had come back a little later, ... and they were all in, bright eyed, right here at 8 o'clock in the morning. School starts at 9:00. At 8:30, I walk in the classroom, there's about 10 of them in there, complaining that Christmas break was too long. 'It should only be a week. We're out for a week.' They missed it here. It's their family, right?

Leo reminded his staff about the serious issues his students often faced that impeded their ability to succeed:

> for some of these kids, they need a warm place where they can have some food and socially interact. Right, so they need the reminders ... They need the reminder of that, and it's a tough one. And I remember being the teacher and when you're trying to focus on 20 kids in the class, or 15, or whatever it is, it's hard to remember those little things that are going on behind the scenes with these kids. So with some of these kids, it is, give them a warm place and try to help them get through these troubled few years in their life.

Terry prioritized creating "a learning environment and a learning community that ... is a healthy, vibrant living organism." His alternative programs built in flexibility so his students had the necessary support to re-engage with school. Successful alternative schools fostered caring atmospheres and positive environments that encouraged student success, evidenced by increased graduation rates and student satisfaction.

Staffing. John believed "that you need to have a team that is working on the same page, you need to have expectations for every kid and that's your starting point." Having flexible, innovative people on staff with a natural aptitude for building relationships with at-risk youth was cited as being a crucial aspect of delivering successful alternative programs. Participants wanted multi-dimensional people with relationship-building abilities, vocational experience and the right mindset to work in their alternative schools. Terry specifically wanted people who were familiar with social services and willing to work beyond their comfort zones. He sought out people with a history of advocacy, volunteering and an understanding of community-based social services. Terry contended that:

There are some people who are the most amazing physics teacher in the world ... But, to put him in a different situation, such as alternative ed., they would not be the best teacher in that environment. So when I say 'best' I mean what is going to be best in this environment with the clients that we're working with to meet their needs because we need very specific traits and characteristics amongst our staff to meet the needs of the students we're working with... As I said earlier who are the best people to work in this environment? Well, they may not be the best math teacher or the best physics teacher that needs to be here, not that I don't have some of those people. I mean if you can have it both, you're in gravy. But, if I have to make a choice, I'm making a choice for the person who is best suited for this type of an environment, who has a willingness to work on the edge of chaos, who has a willingness to go outside their comfort zone and push the boundaries and push the limits at all times, each and every day, who wants to be part of a team... and personality traits. I would wrap it all into one. Who is it I'm looking for? I'm looking for somebody who believes their job is to work with youth, not curriculum, not subject areas, but who believes our job: we teach kids, we teach youth, that's our job. Not math, not science, so I need people who see beyond the standard curriculum. I need people who have an ability to be empathetic ... to understand where's that student coming from ... 'But let me tell you about the work we do. ... Can you work within an advisor program? Can you be part of our team? ...How do you work with youth care workers? How do you work with EA's? ... have you had any experience working with mental health in the community? Have you had any experience working with MCFD, in working with social workers and probation officers? And do you understand that whole other piece?' And sometimes I get blank looks going like 'I'm a math teacher. What are you

92

asking? I'm not a counsellor' ... 'I didn't ask if you were a counsellor. I asked if you understood all these areas and have you had any experience and how can you bring that to bare here?' ... Some maybe intuitively have the character and the personality and the understanding and the empathy, but haven't got the other formal training piece and so I think that that would be the ideal is that you have people who intuitively have that- the art part of working with high-risk youth... some maybe intuitively have the character and the personality and the understanding and the empathy... So, I'm looking for some pretty multi-talented people who have personality traits that one, will reflect the needs of our students; people who can build relationships.... I'm looking for people who are multi-talented, who aren't just good at this, because usually in alternative programs, I don't have the luxury of having 50 or 100 people on staff. Usually our programs are much smaller staffed. And so, I need people who can do multiple things ... So I'm looking for multi-dimensional people because I'm only going to have so many staff and I'm going to have all these students ... And how am I going to meet, what I've said earlier, all these individual needs of these students with this staff?

Relationships. The ability to build relationships with at-risk youth and their families was cited as an alternative educator's most valued skill. An alternative program's ability to create a welcoming atmosphere hinged on this crucial ability to foster caring relationships. Leo recalled that it was initially his ability to connect with at-risk students that garnered the attention of his superiors. Specifically, he emphasized the importance of building relationships with *all* students:

It takes a unique teacher to work with these types of kids. So, I'm always looking at T.O.C.'s and how well do they deal with situations here. How much do the kids like them? Alright, if I have a T.O.C. in and the kids say

"Don't ever bring that *^#&@ back" then I make a call, and (chuckle) they generally don't come back.

In particular, Leo shared his interpretation of the 3 R's:

Some people say relationship, relationship, relationship; for me, it's really relationship, respect, and then relationship. Again, if you can create a respectful environment for the students and foster relationships where they feel comfortable being here, everything else will just, just happen ... Gosh! It's all, gosh ... you hear it so often: It's the relationship. They got to be able to build a relationship, not with 50% of the class, 60, 80, a 100% of the students. All of them, we have to build that ... relationship with them. And if they can't, in my mind, they don't belong here... They really don't. And being respectful, you know, I've had had staff who have come here and transitioned back to regular because they...They couldn't do it. They couldn't build a relationship. They couldn't be respectful with everybody. It's really hard to bite your tongue sometimes. When a kid is saying 'F you, F you, F you' all the way out the building.

Leo shared an example of an English teacher who caught the Ministry of Education's attention because her students consistently outperformed others on their provincial exams. Ministry of Education representatives were curious about this statistical anomaly and sent an observer to this teacher's classroom. They discovered that:

She connected with every kid. There wasn't a day that went by that she didn't say 'hi' to a kid. And often would say, dig a little. 'How was the basketball game on the weekend?'... 'How's your sister doing? I heard she was sick.' Right? Yeah! She got to know the kids. So the kids ... because of that relationship really strong relationship, they worked that extra bit harder, right? And I share that with the staff here. And I mean you connect really well with these kids, they will bend over backwards for you, they will. I guarantee it!

John concurred that relationship-building was paramount: "it's about relationships but it's about relatability as well." He believed that people needed to "recognize the character of the students that we get and ... continue to support what is successful in alternative education." He further reflected that:

It's all about relationships and it's so dramatic in our setting. It's such an obvious thing in our setting, all about relationships... it's dealing with the individual and the individual's needs and being flexible and understanding their situation and building relationships... that's what it's all about, building relationships and finding our kids 'wanna' ... I say it all the time; it's not rocket science working with these kids; it's way the hell more difficult ... to be successful... being honest with those kids.

Terry underscored the importance of building relationships with at-risk youth:

We're the alternative programs. We exist to meet the needs of those students who aren't functioning in that other environment, that need the time for us to build those relationships, heal the wounds, do what is necessary to get them to the stage where they can start moving forward.

As a result, with regards to staffing, Terry felt that: "If they can't build relationships, I don't want them. They are not going to work well here. They are not going to meet the needs of our students."

Staffing challenges. The power of collective agreements to determine staffing assignments frustrated Leo:

You always get kids that will come in and they get a hate on for women or they just hate men because of something that happened in their past and unless you got that balance, and unfortunately we're locked with the

95

way the unions work. I have no control over that. If [union] member X wants to come and be here and they've got the seniority, they get the job. There's no interview, there's no nothing. They don't consider anything about suitability, nothing like that ... And I don't know what the answer is there. I know some districts have gone to more of a contract-base and it works very well for them. They just don't do it here. We're locked into the ... union.

John addressed the impact budgetary constraints had on staffing decisions:

if I get a chance to do some staffing change this year ... part of it revolves around being really flexible and, and maybe I don't need a full-time senior math/science teacher, I need a half-time senior math/science teacher on-site and who is also a half-time DL senior science and math teacher as well. So any saving that I can pick up in staffing that way, then I would apply it to a clerical person to let Jack run this program ... keep all his obligations here and download all the clerical, paper-trail kind of stuff right.

Terry advocated for staffing his alternative programs with "the best" people:

We are professionals, we're not widget makers, we're not assembly line workers, we're professionals who mold a whole pile of variables together to try to move towards an outcome. That's what makes us different. If it was simple, we'd have Zippy the Chimp doing this. You can't. And that's why, again, I say when you're dealing with the most at-risk, marginalized kids in our system, you've got to have your best people doing it because they're the ones who actually have a chance of making that happen.

Participants argued the importance of staffing alternative programs with the 'right people' with the right background, mindset and skill set to operate an

96

alternative program that actually supported its students by building relationships that facilitated meeting their needs.

Vocational certifications. People with vocational certifications, in addition to their university degrees and teacher certifications were seen as highly desirable candidates for alternative education. John remarked that: "the ones that are attracted to us are basically those that are, in addition to being a certified teacher; they're a geologist, and a certified red seal certified baker, people that have done stuff outside of school." In particular, John credited having teachers and support workers who were multi-dimensional and multi-talented as an important reason his schools could offer a woodworking shop that produced guitars and long-boards, an Adventure Education program that brought students on white water rafting field trips and a possible new program certifying students in First Aid/Ski patrol. When given the opportunity, these participants elected to hire teachers and support staff that also had vocational certifications.

Goals, Graduation Plans and Transitions

Traditional high school Dogwood diplomas, adult graduation diplomas and Evergreen school completion certificates are pathways to graduation and school completion in BC. However, only alternative schools could offer evergreens or adult graduation options. The Evergreen certificate primarily focussed on literacy enhancement, numeracy upgrading and work experience opportunities. Leo detailed the graduation plans, noting major changes in 2004 and 2011 that impacted at-risk students' ability to graduate:

So back in 2004, they came out with ... the 2004 Grad which changed ... what we do considerably in alt ed. Cuz the 1995 grad that they operated on before was only 13 courses towards graduations: Grade 11 and 12. They didn't look at any grade 10, it wasn't required. And then in the grade 11 and 12 years, the only mandatory provincials were the grade 12 level provincials. So our kids were fortunate, the only one they really had to write was English 12 or Comm. 12 ... Cuz the rest were electives ... That all changed and went to 20 courses in the 2004 grad which then included grade 10. So grade 10, you need 6 mandatories, P.E. being one of them. P.E. was never part of the program, and then in addition to that, 4 mandatory provincial exams at the grade 10-11 level. Science 10, English 10, Math 10 and Socials 11.

As a result, if his students were seeming unable to meet the traditional Dogwood diploma requirements in their final year of secondary schooling, Leo suggested they work towards an 'adult graduation' diploma: "we'll work on the full grad but as you approach 18 and 19, we're gonna steer you towards something called an adult grad. Adult grads are a lot more manageable than a regular grad."

Learning plans. In accordance with BC's alternative education policy, every student had an Individual Education Plan (IEP) or Student Learning Plan (SLP). These personalized learning plans were meant to ensure students received relevant educational services designed to meet their needs, capacities, interests and talents. These plans included goals addressing basic needs such as housing, physical and mental health issues, in addition to academic goals, behavioural supports and post-secondary planning. For example, Leo remarked:

So everybody does have a plan in the building, and it is very individualized. I have got a kid who comes 20 minutes, twice a week. That's all he can handle. He hasn't been in school since he was in grade 2; kind of the system failed him. He just got out of 'juvee' so that's the best we/he can handle, and that's great. And, on the other end of the spectrum, I've got kids that come every day, all day, 4, 5 hours and they do fine with that, and it works for them. And we can create the program anywhere in between.

Personalized plans were designed to address the needs of each student by providing a customized education a mainstream setting could not offer. For some students, the goal was to be able to "read an application form, fill out an application form, read a newspaper" while other students needed to complete their high school diploma. Leo qualified that:

as you walk up the stairs, we've got a big banner that says "Opening pathways to success" and those pathways can be anyway. Some of the staff here say: 'you're focussed on graduation.' I don't care about graduation, I care about the kids getting on and being successful after they leave here. And if graduation is that step for them, great! If it's me getting them a work experience that turns into a part time of full time job, fantastic! It's whatever are means to each kid! So each kid has an individual program.

Evergreen certificate. Students who were unable to meet traditional or adult graduation requirements received Evergreen school completion certificates. The Evergreen certificate focussed on employment readiness, life skills, literacy and numeracy upgrading. Participants utilized the Evergreen certificate as a last resort. John elaborated that:

you read that file pretty carefully and determine that's an Evergreen school completion bound student and it's no secret to everybody, the parent especially, that's the way the kid will be graduating here and they graduate when they meet the goals of their IEP ... Ours is a handful of Evergreens every year, if that, yeah, small number.

Leo agreed:

we try not to use the Evergreen Certificate too often. The only time we will use it is if we're dealing with a literacy kid that's just not capable ...

Yeah, we don't give out many. Last year, I think I did one. This year we've got a handful of kids targeted. So, I'll hold onto the kids, generally until they're 19 and part of their Evergreen plan, their goals would be meeting a certain literacy level and attending the numeracy classes to get their basic math skills up, addition, subtraction, multiplication, division, just the basic, basic math, and then trying to get some work skills into them, and work experience.

Leo indicated that Aboriginal students comprised a high proportion of Evergreen plans:

A lot of our First Nations kids, we try to get them connected with programs to try. They've got Blade Runners, a few other programs, employment programs that they do ... one of our counselling agencies in town runs a 10 week program, three points in the year, where they take kids and actually pay them. They get $40 a day, I think, to get employability skills to prep them for a job. That's another place we'll steer kids when they're in the last, last months with us. It's a fabulous opportunity to kind of segue into the work world.

Leo further conceded that some students were not interested in graduating:

we've got some kids who they're pretty straight up: 'I don't really care about graduating. I just kind of want to get a job. Help me get a job.' And I always push, 'You graduate and it's going to help you get a job.' But for some of them, 'let's get you into a vocational training program, ACE-IT.'

Post-secondary transitions. Terry noticed an increasing number of students returning to the alternative school in the Fall to upgrade their math or English. Although he understood the need to upgrade, this pattern caused him to pause and reconsider his school's post-secondary transition planning:

one of the things we start seeing was, we had students who never wanted to leave. We had students who would finish their graduation at 18 or 19 or 20 who would be back on our doorstep the next fall, saying 'yeah, well I want to upgrade my math.' Okay, that's great. Okay, we would do that, but why? Why- and/or 'I'm not quite done that or I'm here because I want to get into that college program, so I want to go from Comm. 12 to an English 12.' All good stuff, but we also realized that one of the things that was happening was, for the first time in their lives, they'd found a place they felt comfortable. They found a place where they were safe. They had relationships here that met Maslow's hierarchy and belonging.

The Dogwood, adult and Evergreen graduation plans were available pathways for students in alternative schools. Each student's learning plan was tailored to meet their needs. Work experience, literacy and numeracy upgrading were core components of the Evergreen plan.

Participants Reflections on Outcome and Process

Outcomes in the mainstream public education system were measured by counting course credits and calculating graduation rates. In alternative education, although course credits count for most students, other outcomes are measured according Individual Education Plan's (IEP) or Student Learning Plan's (SLP) goals. Leo noted that student plans ranged from: "'Let's get you graduated,' right? And others, it's the process 'Let's keep you safe here.'" Terry explained that the needs of students attending alternative programs were vastly different than their mainstream counterparts. He contended that processes focussed on students' basic physiological and psychological needs produced better outcomes down the road

you have to have the process to have the outcomes; one is not mutually exclusive to the other. If you don't have the process, outcomes become

accidents; outcomes are just guesswork, outcomes are surprises and we ...
should have less of those in the education system.

Terry advocated that patience and certain processes were required to
support, stabilize and prepare students to engage with their learning:

> All the tools that we can throw at them, we're throwing at them. All of a
> sudden that's making progress and then the final stage and is- I call it the
> race to graduation- where Johnny and his advisor come in and the advisor
> says you know "Mr Terry, Johnny has just told me something and
> Johnny, do you want to tell Mr Terry?" "Well Mr Terry, I want to
> graduate this June." And I'm thinking, okay, a year and a half ago, two
> years ago, when Johnny came, we just wanted to keep Johnny alive and
> now we're at a stage where Johnny's telling me he wants to graduate.
> What has happened? Well, what has happened is a whole pile of work.
> Okay, addressing the things that have to be addressed with Johnny. And
> now, we've got enough money in the bank and we've got enough
> capacity and we've got enough of the lower levels of Maslow's hierarchy
> being met that we're up there hovering around self-esteem, self-
> actualization. We're not going to stay there, cuz sometimes we're going
> to take a step down or two, but we're there. And then all of a sudden,
> Johnny ... becomes one of these kids ... who we're planning for... And
> then I got the guys out there who aren't even on our radar screen but all
> of a sudden, they emerge from that second stage of development and it's
> ... May and some advisor walks in and says "Mr Terry, I think Fred here,
> I think he can make it this year and I know we only got three weeks left,
> but like he hasn't been on my radar screen but all of a sudden, it's like the
> pieces have all started to come together and the math that we thought was
> gonna take another six months, he's just been burning it up the last few
> weeks, the English.

John also noted that although some students "are stepping up to the plate and doing their government exams and having good success rate" others needed to work on developing "as much improved self-esteem and self-respect and employment readiness." Overall, regardless of whether students were on an IEP or SLP, or whether they were working on a Dogwood or adult graduation plan, or Evergreen school completion plan, proper practice had process built into each plan to facilitate short, medium and long term outcomes.

Student success and program efficacy. Participants envisioned measuring student success by using relevant goals, benchmarks, and targets customized in their personal learning plan designed to address their circumstances, needs and interests. In particular, Terry teased out the nuance between effective and successful alternative programs. He argued that measuring measure student success and evaluating program efficacy required the use pertinent benchmarks relevant to alternative students and programs:

There's people within the larger system who would say ... you're not successful unless you're graduating kids; you're not successful unless you've got kids finishing courses, etc. And those are the traditional data that we collect. I think again, we have to do a better job of looking at the data we collect ... So, you have to identify what are those goals? And so you have to be much broader in understanding what those goals are. So if the goals are very narrow, that it's only about graduation and it's only about graduation within five years or six years, well, we're not going to look very successful because we may be very effective in moving our students towards different goals, but we're not very effective at that goal within that time range. So ... in order to be successful, we need to set goals that are realistic and targets that are needed and this target over here might be that we need to get social responsibility skills, we need to develop empathy, we need to develop an understanding of how literacy

103

skills etc. If I have a student that comes to me that's at a grade 2 or 3 level, and in 2 or 3 years, I've got him functioning at a grade 8 or 9 level, we've been very effective to get him to there but if our benchmark for success is grade 12, we're seen as not successful. So, to me, your effectiveness and your success have to be aligned. You have to set targets that mean something, collect data that means something and then judge your effectiveness ... the thing of success is, now ... we've kept this many kids in school, we have this many students enrolled, we have this many students out of jail, we have this many students alive, we have this many students (snap fingers) who are mentally much healthier than they were, physically much healthier than they were, more socially responsible, all these indicators of what is quote 'success.'

Benchmarks such as student-retention, engagement and satisfaction, increased literacy and numeracy levels, stabilized personal lives and improved physical and mental health were suggested. Terry illustrated that:

Maybe 2 years from now, or 3 years from now, or 6 months from now, I might have Johnny to the point where he's coming all day. But I need to be flexible enough that Johnny can survive within my system without getting turfed out.

Terry was adamant that alternative education programs:

cannot be held under the same microscope because we're not dealing with the same clients. And that's a constant process and you have to find different ways of generating different data ... if our programs are going to be judged purely on the five year grad rate, then right off the bat, you've sunk us because very few, if any, of our graduates are going to be within five years. And even the six year rate is going to be- have limited numbers because a student has floundered in the educational system for years.

John agreed that success was individual to each student:

It's how they leave here, whether they transition back to the regular school or how they leave here. What's their resume, what's it filled with, what's their own personal social-emotional inventory of successful experiences ... that's a really important part of it so they can take what they've done here and ... becoming a good employee or go on to some kind of post secondary training... that's how we would measure success, just where the kid started and where they ended up ... when they leave here that they're gonna be contributing individuals, right. And we've seen their success all the time.

When evaluating student progress, Leo considered broader achievements:

What is success? We've talked about it, how it's different for everybody. But for me, the biggest indicator of success with the kids that come back, right, the kids that come back at 20, 25, 30, 35 years old to say: 'Hey thank you. You know *you made a difference*. I didn't graduate. I was an ass hole when I was here (laugh) but you did make a difference, thank you' and those are, those are just huge. And we do get them all the time.

Evaluating Alternative Education Summary

Research question two asked: How does one measure student success and evaluate program efficacy in alternative schools? Findings revealed a number of factors influenced alternative programs' ability to effectively support student success. Factors included supportive leadership, advocacy, adequate funding, staffing attributes and abilities, and finally school climate. Participants discussed their varying degrees of influence over these essential elements.

Participants discussed the importance of measuring student success according to their individual goals. Findings demonstrated that alternative schools offered three school completion options including traditional and adult graduations. Evergreen school completion plans for students who could not graduate encompassed a host of employability readiness preparation.

Reflections revealed the importance of process to achieve outcome; talking the time to stabilize at-risk students to increase the chance of achieving successful outcomes. Evaluating alternative program efficacy also required establishing meaningful goals and relevant benchmarks to assess program performance. Indicators included improved literacy and numeracy, physical and mental health, job readiness skills, emotional literacy, community engagement, quality of life, etc.

21st Century Learning and Alternative Education

The third research question asked: What existing approaches and/or theoretical models make alternative education viable within the 21st Century Learning paradigm? Participants recalled their initial experiences in alternative education, discussed models and practices featuring an advisement system, explored creative pedagogical practices including the use of community partnerships. Findings revealed flexibility and autonomy, personalized learning plans, experiential education and service learning as desired alternative school features.

Findings revealed that successful alternative program models and effective alternative school practices mirrored the goals and principles of 21st Century Learning.

Alternative Education History

Leo recalled his school district's first alternative program:
in '84, our very first one in 1984, a very small one. Alternate ed. in this district started off with 15 kids, two teachers and three support staff, right? It was like a 16 to 19 program. Then it grew. In 1992, they opened this building up, and then that program went to a younger age and so it

exploded from there. Now we've tipped the scales, I think our most we've ever had is 330 kids ... right now we average around 280 to 300.

Terry critiqued the old "warehousing model" (type II) of alternative programs and the old "assembly line model" of education for mainstream schools as being outdated and ineffective. He suggested public opposition to the recommendations of the year 2000 (personalized learning) 'forced' the Ministry of Education to recede to a "back to the basics" approach to education. Terry understood that evidence, research and educational philosophy had advanced beyond the public's comfort zone regarding public education. The same recommendations from the year 2000 were reconfigured in the current 21st Century Learning paradigm.

Alternative Education Features and 21st Century Learning

Terry reflected on 21st Century Learning, the ebbs and flows of educational philosophy and the inherent tension between the public education system's need to change, the economic and political agendas driving those changes and the public's perception of it all:

I mean obviously education is an interesting endeavour. I've often said that education, generally, is reactive. And that's because education is a norm within our society and everybody has their own experiences within that norm. 'This is what education should be, it worked for me, it worked for my grandfather' etc., 'why doesn't it work today?' etc. So, making change to that endeavour is very challenging and usually can only be changed that's within the comfort zone of society. The year 2000 is a good example of that. I mean we had the Sullivan commission in 1988, the Royal Commission on Education. Out of the Sullivan Commission came 83 recommendations. At about that same time, there were some innovative things happening. I was a principal of a junior high school and

107

we were ... involved in team teaching and looking at advisement programs, looking at ways to connect with students; some good, all good stuff. ... Out of the Sullivan Commission came the year 2000 which essentially was trying to look at the recommendations of Sullivan and there were many pieces of that. The year 2000 was a fairly, what I would call for the education system, revolutionary approach to it. Unfortunately- and I was one and many others who embraced many of the philosophical premises of the year 2000 which was to be more student-centered, which was to meet the needs of each individual student which was to get away from some of the industrial assembly line models of education that our system in North America's been based on for decades. So, but unfortunately what happened was, in my reading of it is that it got ahead of the comfort zone. And so you had the public started to go 'well I sure as hell don't want my kid educated that way cuz that's way different than what I know and I know that it worked. What about the 3 R's?' And so- and then of course that translates to trustees and they take heat and board offices take heat and the Ministry takes heat and over a course of 3 or 4 years, maybe 5 or 6 or a little more, there's a pulling back. So we kind of stepped out of the box, we stepped out of our comfort zone to make some significant changes, we got our knuckles wrapped ..., and then you had this reaction to 'back to the basics' again. ... you watch the cycles in education and that's not dissimilar to what's happened before: You had the sixties and you open classrooms and 'we're going to do this and we're going to do that' and then all of a sudden, there's a couple that don't work that well and people don't like and there's the implementation dip and then people ... pull back to what we know and the walls go back up and then we go back to the basics and then we go along again and along comes the year 2000 and we're starting to do all these innovative things and then 'bang' we're back to the basics. ... Now of course, we're moving into PL21... So, again, people get worried 'this is just another trend'... And I go 'no, I don't look at it that way.' I look at it as 'here's another professional development opportunity'... and as professionals, we're not going to take that 'wholis-bolis' and lock-step and apply it. That's not how it works. We're gonna take from it the good things that we think are going to meet the needs of our students and we're going to take the good things from this idea and the good things from that old idea and we're going to create a learning environment and a learning community that again is a healthy, vibrant living organism.

John commented that it just may be time for mainstream schools to consider delivering personalized education, even though it was "fraught with challenges." In fact, John's superintendent commented that:

you guys have been doing it forever and so have shop teachers and it's so true. I mean, we have never, in two school districts the programs that I've been associated with have never been band-aids. They've always been really innovative stuff... mainstream can learn a lot from what we're currently doing. And somehow we need to build into mainstream the flexibility that we have to be involved in these different kinds of initiatives... what is needed if we're gonna be true to the direction that the Ministry of Education is moving in terms of meeting every kid's need and really understanding what it means, PL21 means, individualized instruction, that mainstream has to learn from alternate. Mainstream has to embrace some of the approaches and ideas that we're doing in the province.

Leo's superintendent remarked that "maybe we need to be looking to Leo and his programs as models of how we can change our systems to better meet the needs of all of our kids." Terry was approached by his superintendent 15 years ago to spearhead changes for his district's alternative programs, well before 21st Century Learning materialized. He continued to push the limits of educational paradigms, and 21st Century Learning was no exception:

> And so we're advocating with the district right now for some very innovative programming around meeting their needs and partnership with the community, school-based, or community-based programs and this is where we're now pushing that limit of PL21 and what we're doing around personalizing education... So, again, that's happening on a daily basis here and that's a big push of ours right now, we're hitting some road blocks, because again, we're pushing paradigms and people are getting- are not comfortable with it. My staff is comfortable with it. We know what we need to do, we know who these students are and we need the resources to be able to do it and those resources are going to be different than previous resources... any alternative program worth its salt is doing that every day. That it's not new... It's what we are doing each and every day which is truly personalizing education, not just individualizing. *Individualizing is a strategy; personalizing is a philosophy.* It is an all-encompassing set of principles by which you operate.

Advisement system. Terry implemented an advisement system that facilitated connections and relationships between staff and students, therefore creating a system holding the school accountability for each student's success. He argued that advisory programs provided a formal avenue to meet the needs of students by connecting them to an advisor, building relationships and having a staff person responsible for their learning plan. Terry grounded his advisory model in Maslow's hierarchy of needs, prioritizing physiological needs over academic and/or vocational plans. Terry shared the moment he knew he had to establish this advisement system:

110

One of the things that struck me when I first arrived in our alternative programs; I would have a conversation with teachers about students. And I would ask "tell me about Johnny" and I'd get these blank looks ... So, there wasn't a connection. But nor was there a system in place to get him connected or to get staff connected to him ... And so, the advisement system is something we probably spent five-six years and have continued to work on, but it became the cornerstone that every single student who enters our program has to have an advocate; has to have somebody who's going to go to battle for that kid to meet their needs. And sometimes go to battle with me. I need somebody sitting here in my office advocating for that kid. ... I need somebody over there telling me ten reasons; one reason why we need to keep that kid and ... that had to be built into the system ... So, we're at a stage now, 15 years later, where you can go to anyone of our staff and ask them to talk about their advisees and they will tell you where they come from, what schools they went to, who their parents are, who their social worker is, how long they've been on probation, what counselling they've had, who's working with them, what are their social-emotional needs, where are they at in their grad plan and we do that- we built a system in place within our programs where not only is that reviewed every term. Every term I sit down with each advisor and our youth care work team and we talk about every single kid, and they tell us- and that reflects into our reporting period and also our contract reviews. That's a really important piece but it's a benchmark.

Leo followed suit implementing Terry's advisement model at his alternative school: "I stole... Terry out there is brilliant!" In Leo's district, advisors were responsible for "between 15 and 22 kids that they're supposed to track and maintain contact with the parents."

Flexibility, autonomy and personalized learning. Alternative education has been operationalizing personalized learning well before the advent of the 21st Century Learning paradigm. John, Leo and Terry stated their alternative schools and programs implemented a continuous intake policy and gradual entry options. Their staff personalized student plans, designed innovative programs and tailoring these according to funding availability and staffing options. John noted that:

> It's all about that individualized approach, and there's no cookie cutter approach. We have very clear expectations for codes of conduct that fit our younger and older kids, but it's dealing with the individual and the individual's needs and being flexible and understanding their situation and building relationships. That's the whole, that's what it's all about, building relationships and finding our kids 'wanna' and pulling in whatever kinds of families they have, and working with those families.

Individualizing education and personalizing learning meant that John's school offered a range of programs including early intervention, Adventure Education, applied skills and self-paced courses. John's school embraced experiential learning at its most cutting-edge with river rafting trips, hands-on project learning for kinesthetic students including guitar making and long-board construction, community-based employment opportunities, professional certifications in addition to traditional academic courses.

John cited site location as an important feature contributing the success of alternative students and efficacy of programs. He argued that independently situated alternative schools were better positioned to support at-risk students, allowing his staff more freedom to experiment and flexibility to accommodate students. He felt his programs offered a unique learning experience: "our model of separate as opposed to in-school alternate is necessarily better. I'm totally biased that it is... we've always said the alternate off-site model was better."

Leo's programs were not equipped to serve elementary aged students or offer on-site applied skills courses. However, he pursued community-based opportunities to connect students to work experience options. Leo credited the autonomy and flexibility of his alternative programs and the willingness of his staff to personalize learning plans that supported student's interests, needs and goals. He remarked that learning plans remained flexible and responsive to the changing life circumstances of his students. For example:

It changes daily. Like a kid who maybe we thought we were just focussing on graduation, like the girl who's ... just suddenly stepped right back and we're not even worrying about school now. Let's keep you safe and get you a place to live. She doesn't even have a place to live right now.

Leo wondered whether students would be more amenable to mainstream schools if they could personalize learning to students' interests:

Well, 21st Century Learning, in my mind, what they're doing is they're kind of shifting the system to a more alternate perspective. It's individualized, right? Let's make it work for all the kids. What will the impact be on alternate ed.? I think it have a positive impact because some of the kids who are kind of maybe right on the border of really needing to be here or probably could make it at the high school, maybe will stick it out at the high school because it'll become a little more interesting for them to stay, more individualized.

Terry believed that education should be available and relevant to all students. Students struggling with life issues required more flexibility, support, individualized planning and personalized support. Students in alternative schools presented an array of learning styles, abilities and life issues. Effective programs accommodated their students by tailoring curriculum and pedagogies to their needs, in essence, providing personalized educational services:

It's understanding, okay, today, this is what we got to do. And then it's understanding what are their academic needs and so we've tried to put a fair amount of time in to our approach around assessment and our approach around diagnosing where the student's at and being able to understand that they're functioning at about a two, a grade two reading level. And that if they come in, and sure they're 18, and we're if but we're going to hand them English 12 and say 'yes we have this great environment, it's individual self-paced, you can go as fast as you want, you can go as slow as you want' and we give him English 12 and they're at a two grade two reading level, well they're pace is going to be stopped. And we, and then again, I think, most people in alternate programs would tell you then, three weeks later you're going "where's Johnny? We haven't seen him since he registered" or "he was here, he was a great attender for the first two weeks" and then- well, because Johnny got, just as he did in the regular school, we just did the same thing to him. We created a no-win situation for Johnny and Johnny's frustrated and it's not meeting his needs so why- and it doesn't feel very good, his- now he's had it reinforced to him 'I'm stupid! I'm dumb!'

Terry advocated for the use of multiple pedagogies, beyond simply self-paced work. His ameba analogy exemplified alternative education's ideal flexibility to respond to the needs of students by creating personalized learning plans.

Curriculum, pedagogy and experiential learning. John championed the merits of accommodating curriculum and pedagogical approaches to create personalized learning plans with students. For example, he was a great supporter of interdisciplinary project-based learning:

it's daily exciting to see. You know, why can't project-based learning work? ... in our middle school we have two little, two twins doing the

114

whole of the grade 7 curriculum around horse husbandry, every bit of the grade 7 curriculum around horse husbandry. How do we take that to the next level and make many more of those kinds of projects for many more kids, right?

John believed in student-driven curriculum:

it might be simply focussing weekly on cooking, and then, and then going to another level on that in terms of culinary arts and catering and, and food-safe and pre-employment prep... so you go with that ... and then you do everything in your power to take that kid to that place of reaching their goal, reaching their 'wanna', or ... taking the right steps in that direction.

John illustrated the benefits of experiential learning by describing how the Adventure Education program fostered life skill development in unique settings by engendering collaboration, communication, creative and critical thinking skills. The same reasoning underscored culinary arts and woodworking programs:

it's our shop portable with our woodworking teacher and a child and a male woodworking teacher, male child and youth care worker/bus driver 'slash' and those guys are more into doing basic numeracy and literacy, employment readiness and some entrepreneurial stuff. Like Ricky is a master at building guitars, boats, long-boards. We've got a long-board jig and where they're bumping out the long-boards as good as any factory can make them or better, little, little small, small projects etcetera. ... We're looking, trying to get as much applied skills into them as possible right.

Terry's team developed curriculum, creating 'foundational courses' to address the gap in literacy and numeracy skills:

we have a large number of our students coming to us who are illiterate or have very low literacy skills, very low numeracy skills, so we became one of the ... earliest programs in the province developing the ... new foundation courses around literacy, the seven steps of literacy, the seven steps of numeracy, etc. ... We spent a lot of years developing ... a lot of programs around ... the physical and mental health of our students, and then programs around different learning styles ... so, curriculum, different learning venues, different opportunities for students.

Community partnerships. Community partnerships were an integral component of alternative school efficacy at supporting student success. For example, when John's school district had slated his alternative school for relocation to fill another building in the outskirts of the community, he responded by informing his board and trustees about the successful partnerships his school had developed within the community over the years:

we needed to present the fact that we had very significant community partnerships that were, that are huge! Not the least of which is $17,000 in scholarships and bursaries from many, many, many outside agencies right. But, our... partnership, so I wanted to talk about that but this little vignette was really, really wonderful... It was Teddy and I talking about-, 'cuz, at Christmas we did a dinner, like a gourmet turkey dinner for 125 alone very needy seniors. So we did it ... and it was payback time, like for 10 years of $30,000 right, and that was totally us doing payback.

John exemplified the benefits of both service learning and community partnerships by demonstrating how this relationship had benefited his students as well, including access to the community's "Cadillac of kitchens for your culinary arts program?" He praised how these community relationships were "a beautiful thing! ... a beautiful opportunity to educate people" about the intricate community connections that develop over years.

116

Leo was responsible for eight alternative programs, but unlike John's alternative school, many of Leo's programs were not equipped to offer on-site applied skills initiatives. As a result, he established alliances and partnerships throughout his community. For example:

> ACE-IT opportunities in our district are really growing right now... we are getting more things happening like ACE-IT! We never had ACE-IT kids before. Gosh, this year, we've got, I think we've got about 9 active right now ... We've got 5 girls doing hairdressing right now, we've got plumbing, we've got health care assistant, welding, mechanics. All these kids are out there, carpentry, doing these opportunities which are huge. Now for some of them, that's what they're going to do and they'll do that and they probably won't come back and graduate, and I'm fine with that. If I've helped you get to the next stage in your life then great!

Terry also encouraged his staff to build mutually sustainable relationships to connect students to community resources, social services and work opportunities "what other resources are available in our community, or should be? How can we participate in the development of those resources? How can we support them and then most importantly, how can we work together?" Terry supported business partnerships as well. For example:

> This building you're in was a public-private partnership (PPP) between the school district and our programs and a developer. We designed this building to our specs. The developer paid for it. The enrollments paid, helped the district pay for the program. So you need to understand the business model, you need to understand the realities that school districts face and you need to bring all those things together.

21st Century Learning and Alternative Education Summary

Research question three asked: What existing approaches and/or theoretical models make alternative education viable within the 21st Century Learning paradigm? Findings revealed current alternative program features; systems and models that made alternative schools successful parallel the principles of 21st Century Learning. Participants in this study were strong advocates of personalized learning, autonomous programs, advisement systems, relevant curriculum and innovative pedagogies including experiential learning and applied skills programs. Participants credited flexibility above all else as the cornerstone of successful alternative schools. Community partnerships were identified as a crucial component to successful programs, providing a larger pool of work experience opportunities. For some students, these alliances connected them with community-based resources and social services, while for others; partnerships primed employability readiness and facilitated transitions to post secondary training.

Findings Summary

This study sought to understand and evaluate alternative education, and then compare its heralded features to the 21st Century Learning paradigm. I interviewed three alternative education administrators with extensive experience working in the field. I collected thick and rich narrative data on alternative education philosophy, theory and purpose; student profiles and recent policy development. I learned that alternative programs were a legitimate pathway to high school graduation or school completion that prioritized meeting the needs of their students by adjusting their responses as required.

The findings offered a comprehensive array of factors influencing student success and program efficacy including supportive leadership, advocacy, adequate funding, staffing attributes and abilities, and finally school climate.

Participants discussed student goals, graduation plans and transitions, focussing on the selection of options alternative programs can access for their Evergreen-bound students. Selecting student-centered goals, relevant benchmarks and meaningful targets underscored the importance process played into achieving desired outcomes. Both student success and program efficacy ought to be evaluated according to relevant goals and meaningful benchmarks including improved literacy and numeracy, job readiness skills, emotional literacy, quality of life, etc.

Emergent themes and patterns suggested successful alternative program features, systems and models parallel the principles of the 21st Century Learning paradigm. Characteristics such as personalized learning, engaged and knowledgeable instructors, relevant curriculum, and innovative pedagogies including experiential learning and applied skills programs reflect both alternative education and the tenets of 21st Century Learning. Furthermore, community partnerships connected students with resources and social services, as well as facilitated transitions to post secondary training or employment.

Chapter Five: Discussion

It's simple to chase kids down a hallway with a baseball bat or throw them out of school. It's a lot harder to help them redirect their lives in a positive manner. But, that's what those who work in successful alternative schools do. (Kellmayer, 1995, p. 135)

This study's ultimate aim was to better understand alternative education, how to evaluate its programs and measure its students' success, and subsequently determine how it aligned with 21st Century Learning principles. I conducted a comprehensive literature review and interviewed key informants (Patton, 2002) to explore alternative education's paradigms, policies, programs and practices in this Interpretivist qualitative research design (Crotty, 1998) grounded in phenomenological principles (Giorgi, 1985).

A few key concepts around understanding, evaluating and examining the 21st Century Learning paradigm emerged from the data within the context of the overarching research questions. Alternative schools were created in response to student attrition in the mainstream public education system, as the latter was ill-equipped to support students at-risk of school failure. These marginalized students were usually referred to alternative programs. Given the nature of the clientele, student-centered philosophies were identified as the ideal approach to work with students in alternative programs. Consequently, alternative programs had the flexibility to personalize education to meet each student's needs.

Evaluating programs and students in alternative schools required using a different set of criteria to assess efficacy and measure success. Five and six year graduation rates were poor indicators of program efficacy and student success. Alternative programs were created to capture students falling out of mainstream public schools. As a result, using the same indicators to measure their respective success seemed puzzling. Goals and graduation plans varied from one student to

120

another in alternative education settings. Given that diverse and usually vulnerable students attend alternative programs, evaluation criteria need to capture broader program and student achievements. Alternative schools deliver a vastly different educational service and should be assessed accordingly, as should their students.

Comparing alternative education characteristics, features and models to 21st Century Learning revealed some striking similarities and glaring gaps. Alternative programs found creative ways to deliver personalized educational services to their students, meeting their needs and honouring their interests and talents. In this respect, alternative schools exhibited one of the main principles of 21st Century Learning. However, although alternative programs generally had smaller class sizes, they delivered educational services while being underfunded, under-resourced and/or understaffed. Alternative schools were usually the last ones in a school district to receive current technologies, also a primary feature of 21st Century Learning.

I reviewed these concepts further, based on this study's narrative data and extensive literature review. Foundational themes emerged around understanding and evaluating alternative education, followed by comparing it to the 21st Century Learning paradigm. In this final chapter, I share these reflections, draw conclusions and make recommendations for programs, policy and practice as well as suggest directions for future research.

Understanding Alternative Education

Historically, alternative education programs were initiated in the 1960's and 1970's as innovative educational departures from traditional schooling. With time, alternative schools became marginalized and ghettoized by mainstream schools and society. Students with behavioural designations, learning disabilities, mental health issues, addictions, criminal involvement and other usually poverty-related issues were often referred to alternative programs. Mainstream schools were not designed or intended to make adjustments to personalize education for learners, let alone students requiring extra academic, behavioural and social supports.

Conversely, alternative education programs were established to provide educational services to students who were "pushed out" (Kelly, 1993) of mainstream schools; students who did not fit the system. The type of educational services varied according to the philosophy each program espoused. Vadeboncoeur (2009) argued that school districts provided alternative education for economic benefits such as retaining funding for students who would have otherwise dropped out. In this view, alternative schools acted as an economic safety valve for school districts. Mainstream schools also benefitted from having alternative programs in their districts, as the latter accepted students they suspended, expelled and referred out. Finally, the community benefitted by training students and improving their basic literacy and numeracy to contribute to the local economy by having a job. From an economic standpoint, having people working and contributing to the economy was preferred over having people on social assistance.

From a more holistic standpoint and less cynical perspective, teachers, administrators and associated practitioners agreed that alternative schools existed to meet the needs of their students. Student-centered philosophies dominated the literature pertaining to alternative education (Aron, 2006; Aron & Zweig, 2003; Cable, Plucker & Pradlin, 2009; D'Angelo & Zemanick, 2009; De La Ossa, 2005; Dynarksi & Gleason, 2002; Epp & Epp, 2001; Gamble & Satcher, 2007; Gilson, 2006; Gregg, 1999; Guetzloe, 1997; Hughes-Hassel, 2008; Kellmayer, 1995; Kennedy & Morton, 1999; Kleiner, Porch & Farris, 2002; Lagana-Riordan et al., 2011, Lange & Sletten , 2002; Lange & Lehr, 1999; Meyers, 1998; Oden, 1995; Raywid 1983, 1994, 1997, 2001, 2006; Rix &

Twining, 2007; Sagor, 1999; Shirley, 2010; Van Acker, 2007; Wilkins, 2008; Zweig, 2003). Interestingly, although Raywid (1997) made note that smaller class sizes were more conducive to implementing student-centered approaches, participants did not.

At the heart of these findings, Terry's interpretation of the Starfish analogy, ameba metaphor and village allegory echoed the literature that successful alternative programs purposefully and systemically sought to meet the needs of their students by remaining flexible and personalizing learning plans. The alternative programs in Terry's district were based on Maslow's hierarchy of needs, thus understanding the importance of meeting students' basic needs including housing instability, mental health and addictions and other poverty-related challenges (Aron, 2006; Aron & Zweig, 2003; Cable, Plucker & Spradlin, 2009; Carswell, Hanlon, O'Grady & Watts, 2009; De La Ossa, 2005; Estes, 2006; Gilson, 2006; Guerin & Denti, 1999; ; Jeffries, Hollowell & Powell, 2004; Johnston, Cooch & Pollard, 2004; Johnston & Wetherill, 1998; Kim & Taylor, 2008; Kleiner, Porch & Farris, 2002; Kubic Lytle & Fulkerson, 2004; Lange & Sletten, 2002; Lehr & Lange, 2003; Lehr, Tan & Ysseldyke, 2009; McGee, 2001; Nicholson & Artz, 2008; Payne, 1996; Raywid, 2001; Saunders & Saunders, 2001; Shirley, 2010; Smith, Gregory & Pugh, 1981; Smith et al, 2007; Tissington, 2006; Van Acker, 2007; Vanderven, 2004; Wood, 2001; Zweig, 2003).

Mary Ann Raywid initially articulated that student-centered philosophies accentuated the fundamental belief that each student matters. Raywid's (1994) typology became the seminal reference for alternative educators. This *State of the Art* article was the most frequently cited work in the alternative education literature. This typology classified alternative programs as type I (innovative), II (punitive) or III (remedial) and has been entrenched in academia, alternative education discourse and government policy. Other researchers have expanded this typology, devising a fourth type, to reflect the student-centred philosophies and relationship-based models that have evolved over time (Aron & Zweig, 2003; Henrich, 2005). The BC Ministry of Education embedded student-centered philosophies within its alternative education policy in 2010. This policy stipulated that Type III (remedial) programs would be fully funded if they met the outlined criteria of providing comprehensive services to their students. Therefore, alternative programs that underserviced and warehoused students would not receive comparable funding as fully serviced programs that provide relevant supports to their students.

Closing Thoughts on Understanding

Student-centered philosophies and personalized learning were at the core of successful alternative programs. Students affected by a myriad of personal and socio-economic risk factors populated alternative programs, after having initially tried and failed to succeed in mainstream school settings. Understanding alternative education programs required understanding their clientele and their needs. This understanding resulted in a variety of holistic educational services delivered by alternative schools including supporting students at fundamental levels, meeting their basic physiological and psychological needs. Once stabilized, students could turn to their schooling or vocational training.

In 2010, the BC Ministry of Education crystallized this understating by establishing a policy to govern all alternative education services, protecting and supporting alternative programs that truly operated 'Type III' (remedial) facilities, and not warehousing students. Effective alternative programs worked closely with families and community-based service providers to support students. In short, alternative schools and programs could be defined, described and understood as legitimate pathways to graduation or school completion for students who did not fit the mainstream educational system. Successful alternative programs were more likely to be student-centered and flexible to support students, their needs, interests and goals.

Evaluating Alternative Education

Traditionally, graduation rates and course credits were used to measure student success and determine program efficacy. However, alternative programs delivered a different educational service to a different clientele, therefore should be evaluated using different criteria and benchmarks. Furthermore, a number of external and internal factors influenced alternative schools' ability to be effective in facilitating student success. External factors included funding shortfalls and staffing challenges, while internal factors rested on leadership support and the attributes, abilities, skills and competencies of teachers and support staff.

Alternative education programs measured student success individually, according to their IEP goals or student learning plans. These programs documented their success by using relevant criteria and meaningful benchmarks to assess student progress. These criteria included attendance patterns, emotional development and stability, improved literacy and numeracy, student engagement with job readiness programs, work experience placements and attainment of maturational benchmarks. Some students began attending the alternative program when homeless, suffering from FASD, overwhelmed with mental health concerns, addictions and an inability to read or do math beyond the grade 4 level, and they 'aged out' without graduating. At the end of the programs they achieved an Evergreen school completion certificate filled with accomplishments including successful work experience placements, enhanced job readiness skills and an ability to read at the grade 10 level and do math at the grade 9 level. Were those students not successful at achieving their goals of improved literacy, numeracy and job readiness? Was that program not effective at moving students from where they started to where they ended up? The question was not whether these students' were successful or program effective, but *how* was this program effective at improving these students' life chances and *how* should the system assess this success and be evaluated accordingly?

Based on this example, it became clear that using traditional data (graduation rates and course completions) would not reflect student success or program efficacy. Measuring student success in alternative programs needed to stretch beyond counting course credits and calculating graduation rates. Improvements in literacy, numeracy, employment readiness, mental health, social and civic responsibility and other life milestones needed to be considered and measured. Consequently, a key theme emerged around the districts' need to evaluate students in alternative education differently, using meaningful indicators and relevant benchmarks to measure their success.

External factors that influenced alternative programs' ability to provide adequate education services included staffing challenges, funding shortfalls, local and provincial political decisions. External factors played an integral role in the success or failure of alternative programs and, *de facto*, their students. For example, funding considerations had great influence over program capability, as funding sources were often unstable, unpredictable and unreliable (Atkins, Bullis & Todis, 2005; Jeffries, Hollowell & Powell, 2004; Nicholson & Artz, 2008; Raywid, 1996). Administrators relied heavily on the ability to apply and secure grants to supplement their resource budgets.

Staffing programs with multi-dimensional caring people who had a natural ability to develop relationships with all at-risk youth and establish welcoming environments in their programs was cited as paramount. Staff attributes including relationship building abilities and other human qualities were identified as cornerstones of successful alternative programs. These

126

findings echoed the literature's stance regarding the importance of staffing alternative programs with multi-talented people who had exceptional relationship-building skills. Teachers in alternative education played multiple roles throughout the day; they were counsellors, advisors, coordinators, teachers, friends, etc. (Atkins, Bullis & Tobis, 2005; Jeffries, Hollowell & Powell, 2004; Kellmayer, 1995; Raywid, 1982, 1996; Saunders & Saunders, 2001).

The most significant finding, also echoed by the literature, was the value alternative programs placed on teachers and support workers with exceptional relationship-building abilities (Castaneda, 1997; De La Ossa, 2005; Fallis & Opotow, 2003; Jones, 2011; Magee-Quinn, Poirier, Faller, Gable & Tonelson, 2006; Owens & Kondol, 2004; Poyrazli et al., 2008; Raywid, 1982; San Martin & Calabrese, 2011; Wilkins, 2008; Wolf & Wolf, 2008; Zhang, 2008). Establishing genuine and authentic relationships allowed staff to meaningfully connect with all students, creating safe and welcoming atmospheres that made them feel at-ease, cared for and supported (Aron, 2006; Aron & Zweig, 2003; Bullock, 2007; Cox, 1999; De La Ossa, 2005; Dupper, 2006; Fitzsimons-Hughes & Adera, 2006; Jeffries, Hollowell & Powell, 2004; Johnston, Cooch & Pollard, 2004; Jones, 2011; Kellmayer, 1995; Kim & Taylor, 2008; Kleiner, Porch & Farris, 2002; Lagana-Riordan et al., 2011; Lange & Sletten, 2002; Lehr & Lange, 2003; McGee, 2001; Magee-Quinn, Poirier, Faller, Gable & Tonelson, 2006; Morrissette, 2011; Owens & Kondol; 2004; Powell, 2003; Poyrazli et al., 2008; Raywid, 1982; San Martin & Calabrese, 2011; Smith et al., 2007; Wilkins, 2008; Zweig, 2003). Students who felt valued and supported were more likely to stay connected to their school program.

The success of alternative schools rested on their understanding of process and the time needed to address the needs of students. In essence, student-centered philosophies were process-driven and supported students towards achieving their goals in meaningful ways. As a result, evaluating alternative programs effectiveness required choosing relevant criteria, and selecting applicable benchmarks to assess program efficacy and student success. There are no outcomes without process. Consequently, a broader range of measures, benchmarks, indicators and methods of measurement were suggested to evaluate the true efficacy of alternative programs. Relevant criteria and milestones generated meaningful data that actually reflected student success and program efficacy (Lange & Lehr, 1999; Lange & Sletten, 2002; Lehr & Lange, 2003; Lehr, Tan & Ysseldyke, 2009; Nicholson & Artz, 2008; Oden, 1995).

Oden (1995) suggested that "outcomes-oriented program evaluations" offered "an insufficient understanding of the content and processes of the approaches or programs they studied" (p. 177). Lehr, Tan and Ysseldyke (2009) urged alternative schools to closely document their successes, "to secure funding and enhance their reputation. Progress indicators in areas beyond academic performance may be necessary to capture the impact of alternative schools on student outcomes" (p. 30). Lehr and Lange (2003) understood that:

> many alternative schools focus on promoting youth development and education across many domains (e.g., social, academic, emotional, vocational), measuring academic progress alone may not capture the richness of what some alternative schools offer and the changes that can occur for youth who attend. (p. 63)

Findings are consistent with the literature in that student success is contingent on a program's ability to effectively deliver innovative educational services which hinge on external factors such as funding and internal factors such a quality and suitability of staff.

Concluding Evaluations

Gregg (1999), Aron and Zweig (2003) and Henrich (2005) compiled tables cataloguing alternative program domains, dimensions and types that could be used as the basis of qualitative evaluations. It is important to remember that upon intake, students were initially "disenchanted disadvantaged and disengaged" from the regular educational system. As a result, alternative schools needed to offer a completely different set of educational services that met the actual needs of students, starting with stabilizing their lives prior to re-engaging them back into school and community. Maslow's hierarchy of needs was the basis of this understanding. Stabilizing at-risk students required time, skill and a coordinated team approach. Time-consuming processes included building relationships, fostering resilience and establishing protective factors to support at-risk students (Brendtro, Brokenleg & Van Bockern, 2002; Kellmayer, 1995; Kelly, 1993).

When adequately funded, resourced and staffed, alternative schools could be as successful as mainstream educational institutions at graduating students and/or preparing them for life beyond high school. Alternative schools understood the needs of their clients and the processes required to meet those needs. Participants strongly suggested their schools, programs and students should be evaluated using relevant criteria. Indicators such as the facilitation of non-educational services, adjusted graduation timelines, personalized learning plans including the development of emotional literacy, developmental milestones and pre-employment skills needed to be measured and accounted for. Student success was assessed in accordance to IEP and SLP goals, course completions, graduation and/or securing employment.

Overwhelmingly, findings suggested that transitioning students back to mainstream schools often destroyed their progress and was counterintuitive to their success. Graduation remained important, but so was improving basic

129

skills, job readiness, physical and mental health. In BC, every alternative student was expected to have a personalized education plan designed to meet their needs, interests and goals. Some students graduated alternative school with a traditional Dogwood diploma, some with an adult diploma and others with an Evergreen school completion certificate.

Comparing Alternative Education and 21st Century Learning

Having come to an understanding about what alternative education was and how it should be evaluated, this final question sought to compare successful alternative program characteristics and approaches against the principles of the 21st Century Learning paradigm.

The findings suggested that alternative programs operationalized 21st Century learning principles for years, and attempted to do so without the top-down paradigm, funding, leadership, resources, staffing or technology. Characteristics of successful alternative schools included program flexibility, personalized learning plans, customized curriculum, project-based learning, diverse pedagogical approaches that promoted the holistic development of its students. Participants prided themselves on their school's ability and willingness to respond to the needs of students by accommodating their circumstances with personalized learning plans that met their needs by adopting a student-centered approach (Starfish analogy) and flexible program (Ameba metaphor).

Successful alternative education programs' 'claim to fame' was their ability to be flexible in every aspect of their programs including attendance, curriculum, learning plans, pedagogy, staffing and so much more. Participants echoed the literature in consistently identifying flexibility as alternative education's greatest strength (Epp & Epp, 2001; Groves, 1998; Jeffries, Hollowell & Powell, 2004; Lange & Sletten, 2002; Smith et al., 2007). Alternative programs enhanced their ability to be flexible by developing

130

community partnerships to support their students. Such alliances included work experience opportunities and job readiness program options. The literature supported these findings, noting the benefits of having access to vocational and work experience opportunities (Aron, 2006; Aron & Zweig, 2003; Carswell, Hanlon, O'Grady & Watts, 2009; Foley & Pang, 2006; Kleiner, Porch & Farris, 2002; Lange & Sletten, 2002; Lehr & Lange, 2003; Long, Page, Hail, Davis & Mitchell, 2003; Platt, Casey & Faessel, 2006; Smith et al., 2007; Zweig, 2003).

When adequately staffed, resourced and funded, most alternative schools were in a position to customize their programs (Gamble & Satcher, 2007), facilitate experiential learning opportunities (McGee, 2001), take students on field trips (Johnston & Wetherill, 1998; Hall, 2007; Raywid, 1982, 1994, 1996, 1997, 2006), provide accelerated courses and develop project-based curriculum (Dynarski & Gleason, 1999) and offer service learning opportunities (Guerin & Denti, 1999; McCall, 2003; Raywid, 1982, 1983; Smith et al., 2007). There were several program models (Kellmayer, 1995; Lange & Sletten, 2002) and dimensions and domains (Duke & Griesdorn, 1999; Fitzsimons-Hughes & Adera, 2006) to consider when designing and evaluating alternative schools. The literature suggested alternative programs refrain from relying exclusively on self-paced course packs to manage the diversity of their student body (Atkins, Bullis & Todis, 2005, Cable, Plucker & Spradlin, 2009; Johnston & Wetherill, 1998; Lange, 1998; McNulty & Roseboro, 2009; Raywid, 1982).

A key finding revealed that alternative schools formed necessary partnerships with community-based social service providers. These alliances were said to be crucial in facilitating student success by supporting alternative programs' student-centered mandate to meet the needs of their students. Kleiner, Porch and Farris (2002) catalogued a list of service providers that collaborated with alternative schools, providing a snapshot of the intricate

131

network of services at-risk students may require: The juvenile justice system, community mental health agencies, police and/or sheriff's department, child protection services, hospital or other health service, community organizations, family organizations, crisis intervention centers, family planning, job placement centers and local parks and recreation departments. Findings and literature overwhelmingly agreed that alternative schools would be greatly disadvantaged without access to community-based supports (Dynarski & Gleason, 2002; Gamble & Satcher, 2007; Raywid, 1982). Having access to these services on site at the alternative school was seen as ideal, but some programs were prevented from having workers in their schools that were not part of the local unions within the school district. Therefore, although alternative programs were considered more effective when acting as a hub of support services for students and families (Aron & Zweig, 2003; Atkins, Bullis & Todis, 2005; Castaneda, 1997; Dynarski & Gleason, 2002; Foley & Pang, 2006; Kellmayer, 1995; Leone & Drakeford, 1999; Long, Page, Hail, Davis & Mitchell, 2003; McGee, 2001), sometimes other contractual complications prevented community-based services from operating on site.

Situations such as these prompted Terry to implement an advisement system in his programs to ensure each student was systemically connected with an adult responsible for overseeing their educational plan. Terry believed that having a meaningful advisement system in place at his alternative school would facilitate student success by capturing at-risk youth, connecting with them and supporting their access to community resources and services.

In this study, alternative education approaches, characteristics and models primarily featured program flexibility, personalized learning plans, customized curriculum, and a diverse menu of pedagogical approaches including experiential and service learning. These features closely resembled 21st Century Learning's vision that:

132

As the student progresses the system needs to allow flexibility that not only accommodates the student's abilities but also engages them by catering to their interests. The student will take a larger and larger role in charting a path best suited to those talents, interests, and abilities. (PTC, 2010, p. 16)

Comparing Paradigms Conclusions

Flexibility and personalized learning were recognized as highly desirable features in successful alternative education programs. By far, these two characteristics featured most prominently across the findings and literature (Aron, 2006, Aron & Zweig, 2003; Dynarski & Gleason, 2002; Kellmayer, 1995; Lange & Sletten, 2002). Alternative schools' willingness to be flexible allowed them to personalized learning plans that were meaningful to students using available curriculum, pedagogy and community supports to meet the needs of their students. Project-based learning, applied skills courses and experiential opportunities were heralded as key pedagogical features in successful alternative programs.

The primary characteristics that made alternative education successful were the same features advanced by the BC Ministry of Education with their 21st Century Learning initiative. With flexible pedagogy and personalized learning plans, alternative schools argued that they have been modelling the 21st Century learning practices for decades. Given that the 21st Century Learning initiative touts personalized learning and flexible pedagogy as key principles to their paradigm (BC Min. of Ed., 2010a; PTC, 2010), in this instance, we could tentatively conclude that, indeed, alternative programs have been operationalizing these principles. The participants argued that alternative education programs and practices could inform the implementation of 21st Century Learning in larger mainstream settings. Providing alternative programs with the technology, resources and staffing to fully implement 21st Century Learning would be an intriguing endeavour.

Strengths and Limitations of the Study

Strengths. My participants have 85 years of educational experience, 63 years of alternative education experience and 47 years of administrative experience in BC. Their experiences provided me with rich narrative data. I honoured the qualitative research tradition by remaining true to the Interpretivist epistemology (Crotty, 1998); wholly engaging in the "InterView" process (Kvale, 1996) and adhering to the principles of phenomenological research (Giorgi, 1985). I meticulously transcribed and analyzed data with the support of a reputable qualitative software application (*NVivo*). This study filled a gap in the literature on alternative education by offering the unique voices of Vancouver Island alternative administrators to the alternative education conversation and by providing an in-depth historical and contemporary perspective that cannot be found anywhere in the Canadian literature.

Limitations. As stated in chapter three, the primary limitation of this study is the inability to replicate it. This research endeavour is qualitative in nature, relying on the experiences, interpretations and perceptions of the participants that are specific to them and their geographic location. A further limitation was the absence of a national database collating educational data across Canada, preventing an international comparison between American and Canadian data. Education falls under provincial jurisdiction in Canada. The final limitation was the complete lack of available female participants for this study. All administrators were male.

Recommendations

Several recommendations emerged directly from the participants, from analyzing the data and from reviewing the literature. Accordingly, I offer the following policy recommendations to the Ministry of Education; governance suggestions for school districts and program-based propositions for alternative education practitioners (see Table 1).

Reassessing funding allocation, student-teacher ratio, class sizes and evaluation criteria are critical in this time of educational change. Informal feedback from participants and other alternative education practitioners highlighted that, although the Ministry of Education might be well-intentioned in wanting to move forward with 21st Century Learning, they will need to let go of traditional educational paradigms. They cannot have it both ways. The Ministry of Education cannot cut funding to school districts and expect them to expand personalized education.

There appears to be a gap between the philosophy of 21st Century Learning, the practical implementation of personalizing education and its funding. These recommendations invite politicians, administrators and practitioners to reflect on how the Ministry of Education, school districts and alternative programs can bridge some of these gaps by using the skills they are hoping their students will graduate with, namely effective communication, collaboration, critical thinking and creativity.

Table 1: Recommendations to improve alternative education services in BC

Recommendations for the Ministry of Education (MOE)
<ul><li>Create a "best practices in alternative education" working group comprised of alternative education practitioners, administrators and researchers to develop a practiced-based and research-informed document to act as a guide for alternative schools;</li><li>Create a program evaluation platform using both relevant qualitative indicators as benchmarks to supplement standard quantitative data;</li><li>Create a useful database or central website of alternative programs for practitioners to encourage them to network and learn from each other;</li><li>Reassess funding allocation and structures to align with 21st Century principles;</li><li>Include students and parents in the evaluative process.</li></ul>
Recommendations for the public school system
<ul><li>Target funding! Allow alternative schools to use the funds generated by their students to support them;</li><li>Reassess overall educational service delivery model to streamline with MOE's 21st Century learning initiative;</li><li>Revisit the interpretation and implementation of collective agreements over staffing matters; develop a process to include suitability as a consideration for employment without solely relying on seniority as a determining factor to fill a vacant posting;</li><li>Study your district's successful alternative programs for ideas on how to implement 21st Century learning in a mainstream setting;</li><li>Restore professional development days exclusively for alternative educators and practitioners;</li></ul>

- Keep class sizes manageable and adequately staffed with educational assistants and other support workers;
- Develop an evaluation protocol to validate, assess and record the process required to move at-risk students forward in their education and personal development;
- Include students and parents in the evaluative process.

Recommendations for schools and programs

- Personalize learning plans according to student needs, capacities and interests;
- Measure student success according to their individual goals;
- Maintain a student-centered approach and believe in the process;
- Be flexible in your attendance policies, program structure and pedagogies;
- Move beyond self-paced worksheets and course packs;
- Develop innovative curriculum and unique pedagogies;
- Foster as many community partnerships as possible;
- Advocate, advocate, advocate for your students and programs;
- Maintain caring relationship and a welcoming atmosphere

Future Research

This study contributed voices from the central Vancouver Island region to the alternative education discourse. I selected alternative education administrators for their unique experience and perspectives regarding alternative education. Future research should invite alternative education students, their parents, teachers and other practitioners to add their voices, lived experiences, thoughts and feelings to the alternative education conversation. Additional qualitative studies featuring alternative education philosophies, programs and practices are needed from different regions and provinces to further inform the Canadian alternative education field. Finally, future research should further explore the relationship between 21st Century Learning and alternative education, as these paradigms are seemingly evolving side by side.

Final Reflection

Alternative education schools and programs have cycled through a number of educational paradigms across North America over the past 50 years. In general, alternative programs have been used as dumping grounds for troubled students and challenging staff. Recently, with continued student attrition and the advent of the 21st Century Learning paradigm, alternative schools have begun to be viewed differently by the Ministry of Education, school districts and researchers.

Tan, Lehr and Ysseldyke (2009) drew attention to the current reality of "meeting the needs of students disenfranchised from the traditional education system is becoming more and more important as we are faced with a growing population of students for whom status quo education is not successful" (p. 19). This reality may have been the impetus the BC Ministry of Education needed to legitimize and validate the work of alternative programs across the province. Furthermore, instead of undercutting alternative programs, perhaps the time has come to adequately fund alternative programs and look to them for innovative ways to personalize learning, thus growing 21st Century Learning in the public educational system.

If a growing number of students are becoming "disenchanted, disenfranchised and disengaged," this could be a direct reflection of the community, economy, society and world we live in. The overall educational system is a microcosm of this world. The 21st Century Learning paradigm's (over)-reliance on technology could entrench a chasm between technological and the ability to effectively communicate and collaborate, and lack the critical thinking skills and confidence to be creative. Alternative programs were rarely adequately resourced compared to their mainstream counterparts when it came to technology. Alternative programs usually received 'hand-me-downs' from mainstream schools. Furthermore, graduation plans and evaluation systems continued to favour the traditional benchmarks of course completions and graduation rates.

Although "fraught with challenges", perhaps mainstream schools could adopt a few characteristics that have well served alternative programs. Student-centered philosophies, personalized learning, student-driven curriculum and diverse pedagogical options facilitated by knowledgeable and caring teachers with adequate resources and supports have allowed alternative programs to find effective ways of facilitating education. These features could be the basis of the 21st Century Learning paradigm taking hold in mainstream schools.

Based on this study, alternative schools had the flexibility to experiment with various approaches, frameworks, philosophies and models that could potentially be extrapolated and adapted to larger educational systems. However, ideas, plans and discourses are one thing, action is another. As Terry said:

> we truly need to 'walk the talk' and make sure that we are truly trying to meet the needs of each individual and truly trying to personalize

139

education if we're going to see the system move forward. And, I think alternative education can be looked at as a great test case for how you can do that as I believe that's where some of that stuff is happening on a daily basis and I think the traditional system can learn from that. It doesn't mean we have it figured out by any means, but getting back to our greatest strength, we've had the flexibility and we've been given the licence to do it, and when that happens, some pretty exciting things can happen when you got the right people.

Upon reflection of this entire research process, and the wealth of knowledge I have been privileged to access and analyze, I am seriously considering publishing these findings in a book to honour the voices of these alternative education practitioners and maintain a living document that fosters a conversation geared towards supporting students who have been discarded by the mainstream educational system.

References

Ansell, J. (2007). At-risk students in transition. *The Canadian Association of Principals Journal: Resources for school-based leadership, 15*(1), 10-12.

Aron, L.Y. (2006). *An overview of alternative education.* Washington, DC: The Urban Institute.

Aron, L.Y. & Zweig, J.M. (2003). *Educational alternatives for vulnerable youth: Student needs, program types, and research directions.* Washington, DC: The Urban Institute.

Atkins, T. (2008). Is an alternative school a school of choice? It depends. *Journal of School Choice, 2*(3), 344-347.

Atkins, T., Bullis, M., & Todis, B. (2005). Converging and diverging service delivery systems in alternative education programs for disabled and non-disabled youth involved in the juvenile justice system. *Journal of Correctional Education, 56*(3), 253-285.

Baumeister, R.F. & Leary, M.R. (1995). The need to belong: Desire for interpersonal attachments as a fundamental human motivation. *Psychological Bulletin, 117*(3), 497-529.

Bazeley, P. (2007). *Qualitative data analysis with NVivo.* Los Angeles: Sage Publications.

Brendtro, L. K., Brokenleg, M. & Van Bockern, S. (2002). *Reclaiming youth at risk: Our hope for the future.* Bloomington, IN: Solution Tree.

Brendtro, L. K., Brokenleg, M., & Van Bockern, S. (2005). The circle of courage and positive psychology. *Reclaiming Children and Youth, 14*(3), 130-136.

British Columbia Alternate Education Association. (2011). What is alternate education? Retrieved from: http://bctf.ca/bcaea/about.html.

British Columbia Ministry of Education (2012). Provincial reports. Retrieved from http://www.bced.gov.bc.ca/reporting/prov_data_summary.php.

British Columbia Ministry of Education. (2010a). 21st century learning. Retrieved from http://www.bced.gov.bc.ca/dist_learning/21century_learning.htm.

British Columbia Ministry of Education. (2010b). Policy document: Alternate education school Program policy. Retrieved from http://www.bced.gov.bc.ca/policy/policies/alt_education_school_program. htm.

Brokenleg, M. (2005). Raising respectful children. *Reclaiming Children and Youth, 14*(2), 85-86.

Bullock, L. M. (2007). Introduction to the special issue: Ensuring student success through alternative schools. *Preventing School Failure: Alternative Education for Children and Youth, 51*(2), 3-4.

Bullock, L. M., & Gable, R. A. (2006). Programs for children and adolescents with emotional and behavioral disorders in the united states: A historical overview, current perspectives, and future directions. *Preventing School Failure: Alternative Education for Children and Youth, 50*(2), 7-13.

Cable, K.E., Plucker, J.A. & Spradlin, T.E. (2009). Alternative schools: What's in a name? *Center for Evaluation and Education Policy: Education Policy Brief, 7*(4), 1-12.

Carpetner-Aeby, T., & Kurtz, P. D. (2000). The portfolio as a strengths-based intervention to empower chronically disruptive students in an alternative school. *Children in Schools, 22*(4), 217-231.

Carswell, S.B, Hanlon, T.E., O'Grady, K.E. & Watts, A.M. (2009). A preventive intervention program for urban African American youth attending an alternative education program: Background, implementation, and feasibility. *Education and Treatment of Children, 32*(3), 445-469.

Carver, P. R., and Lewis, L. (2010). *Alternative Schools and Programs for Public School Students At Risk of Educational Failure: 2007–08* (NCES 2010–026). U.S. Department of Education, National Center for Education Statistics. Washington, DC: Government Printing Office.

Castaneda, L.V. (1997). Alternative to failure: A community-based school program for Latino teens. Education and Urban Society, 30, 90-106. doi:10.1177/0013124597030001006

Castleberry, S.E. & Enger, J.M. (1998). Alternative school students' concepts of success. *National Association of Secondary School Principals Bulletin, 82,* 105-111. doi:10.1177/019263659808260215.

Cox, S.M. (1999). An assessment of an alternative education program for at-risk delinquent youth. *Journal of Research in Crime and Delinquency, 36,* 323-336. doi:10.1177/0022427899036003004

Cox, S.M., Davidson, W.S. & Bynum, T.S. (1995). A meta-analytic assessment of delinquency-related outcomes of alternative education programs. *Crime & Delinquency, 41*, 219-234. doi:10.1177/0011128795041002004.

Creswell, J. W. (2003). *Research design: Qualitative, quantitative, and mixed method approaches* (2nd ed.). Thousand Oaks, CA: Sage Publications.

Creswell, J. W. (1998). *Qualitative inquiry and research design: Choosing among five traditions*. Thousand Oaks, CA: Sage Publications.

Creswell, J. W., & Miller, D. L. (2000). Determining validity in qualitative inquiry. *Theory into Practice, 39*(3), 124-130.

Crotty, M. (1998). *The foundations of social research: Meaning and perspective in the research process*. Thousand Oaks, CA: Sage Publications.

D'Angelo, F. & Zemanick, R. (2009). The twilight academy: An alternative education program that works. *Preventing School Failure: Alternative Education for Children and Youth, 53*(4), 211-218.

De La Ossa, P. (2005). Hear my voice: Alternative high school students' perceptions and implications for school change. *American Secondary Education, 24*(1), 24-39.

Denzin, N. K., & Lincoln, Y. S. (1994). *Handbook of qualitative research.* Thousand Oaks, CA: Sage Publications.

Denzin, N. K. & Lincoln, Y. S. (2000). Introduction: The discipline and practice of qualitative research. In N.K. Denzin, & Y.S. Lincoln, (eds.), *The SAGE handbook of qualitative research* (2nd ed., pp. 1-28). Thousand Oaks, CA: Sage Publications.

Denzin, N. K., & Lincoln, Y. S. (2005). *The SAGE handbook of qualitative research* (3rd ed.). Thousand Oaks, CA: Sage Publications.

Denzin, N. K., Lincoln, Y. S., & Smith, L. T. (2008). *Handbook of critical and indigenous methodologies.* Los Angeles, CA: Sage Publications.

Dreamstime. (2012). Maslow's hierarchy of needs pyramid. Retrieved from: http://www.dreamstime.com/stock-image-maslow's-hierarchy-needs-pyramid-image18682831.

Duke, D.L. & Griesdorn, J. (1999). Considerations in the design of alternative schools. *The Clearing House: A Journal of Educational Strategies, Issues and Ideas, 73*(2), 89-92. http://dx.doi.org/10.1080/00098659909600155

Dupper, D. R. (2006). Guides for designing and establishing alternative school programs for dropout prevention. In C. Franklin, M. B. Harris, & P. Allen-Meares (Eds.), *The School Services Sourcebook: A guide for School-based Professionals* (397–404). New York, NY: Oxford University Press.

Dynarski, M. & Gleason, P. (2002). How can we help? What we have learned from recent federal dropout prevention evaluations. *Journal of Education for Students Placed at Risk (JESPAR), 7*(1), 43-69. http://dx.doi.org/10.1207/S15327671ESPR0701_4.

Epp, J.R. & Epp, W. (2001). Easy exit: School policies and student attrition. *Journal of Education for Students Placed at Risk (JESPAR), 6*(3), 231-247.

Estes, M. (2006). Charter schools: Do they work for troubled students? *Preventing School Failure: Alternative education for children and youth, 51*(1), 55-61.

Fallis, R. K. & Opotow, S. (2003). Are students failing school or are schools failing students? Class cutting in high school. *Journal of Social Issues 59*(1), 103–119.

Feinstein, S., Driving-Hawk, C., & Baartman, J. (2009). Resiliency and Native American teenagers. *Reclaiming Children and Youth, 18*(2), 12-17.

Fine, M., Weis, L., Weseen, S. and Wong, L. (2000). For whom? Qualitative research, representations and social responsibilities. In N.K. Denzin, & Y.S. Lincoln, (eds.), *The SAGE handbook of qualitative research* (2nd ed., pp. 107-131). Thousand Oaks, CA: Sage Publications.

Fitzsimons-Hughes, A. & Adera, B. (2006). Education and day treatment opportunities in schools: Strategies that work. *Preventing School Failure: Alternative Education for Children and Youth, 51*(1), 26-30.

Flower, A., McDaniel, S.C. & Jolivette, K. (2011). A literature review of research quality and effective practices in alternative education settings. *Education and Treatment of Children, 34*(4), 489-510.

Foley, R. M., & Pang, L. (2006). Alternative education programs: Program and student characteristics. *The High School Journal, 89*(3), 10-21.

Fontana, A. & Frey, J.H. (2005). The interview: From neutral stance to political involvement. In N.K. Denzin, & Y.S. Lincoln, (eds.), *Handbook of Qualitative Research* (3rd ed., pp. 695-727). Thousand Oaks, CA: Sage Publications.

Fontana, A. & Frey, J.H. (2000). The interview: From structured questions to negotiated text. In N.K. Denzin, & Y.S. Lincoln, (eds.), *Handbook of Qualitative Research* (2nd ed., pp. 645-672). Thousand Oaks, CA: Sage Publications.

Fuller, C. G. & Sabatino, D. A. (1996). Who attends alternative high schools? *The High School Journal, 79*(4), 293-297.

Gable, R.A., Bullock, L.M. & Evans, W.H. (2006). Changing perspectives on alternative schooling for children and adolescents with challenging behaviour. *Preventing School Failure: Alternative Education for Children and Youth, 51*(1), 5-9.

Gamble, D., & Satcher, J. (2007). A one-room schoolhouse. *Journal of Correctional Education, 58*(1), 14-26.

Gilson, T. (2006). Alternative high schools: What types of programs lead to the greatest level of effectiveness? *Journal of Educational Research & Policy Studies, 6*(1), 48-66.

Giorgi, A. (Ed.). (1985). *Phenomenology and Psychological Research.* Pittsburgh, PA: Duquesne University Press.

Gorney, D.J. & Ysseldyke, J.E. (1992). *Students with disabilities use of various options to access alternative schools and area learning centers. Research report number 3 enrollment options for students with disabilities.* Minneapolis, MN: Minnesota University.

Gregg, S. (1999). Creating effective alternatives for disruptive students. *The Clearing House: A Journal of Educational Strategies, Issues and Idea, 73*(2), 107-113.

Groves, P. (1998). Meeting the needs of 'at risk' students: The day and night school. *The High School Journal, 81*(4), 251-257.

Guba, E.G. and Lincoln, Y. (2005). Paradigmatic controversies, contradictions, and emerging confluences. In N.K. Denzin, & Y.S. Lincoln, (eds.), *Handbook of Qualitative Research* (3rd ed., pp. 191-215). Thousand Oaks, CA: Sage Publications.

Guerin, G. & Denti, L. (1999). Alternative education support for youth at-risk. *The Clearing House: A Journal of Educational Strategies, Issues and Ideas, 73*(2), 76-78.

Guetzloe, E. (1997). The power of positive relationships: Mentoring programs in the school and community. *Preventing School Failure: Alternative Education for Children and Youth, 41*(3), 100-104.

Hall, M. (2007). Mentoring the natural way: Native Approaches to education. *Reclaiming Children and Youth, 16*(1), 14-16.

Heidegger, M. (1982). *The basic problems of phenomenology* (Rev. ed.). Bloomington, IN: University Press.

Henrich, R. S. (2005). Expansion of an alternative school typology. *Journal of At-risk Issues, 11*(1), 25-37.

Holstein, J.A. & Gubrium, J.F. (2005). Interpretive practice and social action. In N.K. Denzin, & Y.S. Lincoln, (eds.), *The SAGE handbook of qualitative research* (3rd ed., pp. 483-505). Thousand Oaks, CA: Sage Publications.

Hughes-Hassell, S. (2008). Alternative educational settings: What can we learn from them? *Knowledge Quest, 37*(1), 8-11.

147

Human Research Ethics Board. (2010). *Annotated guidelines for completing the human research ethics board application for ethics approval for human participation research.* Victoria, BC: University of Victoria. Retrieved from: http://www.uvic.ca/research/assets/docs/ors/forms/ethics/human/Annotated%20Guidelines%20for%20Ethics%20Application.pdf

Janesick, V.J. (2000). The choreography of qualitative research design. In N.K. Denzin, & Y.S. Lincoln, (eds.), *The SAGE handbook of qualitative research* (2nd ed., pp. 379-399). Thousand Oaks, CA: Sage Publications.

Jeffries, R. B., Hollowell, M., & Powell, T. (2004). Urban American Indian students in a non-punitive alternative high school. *American Secondary Education, 32*(2), 63-78.

Johnston, C., Cooch, G. & Pollard, C. (2004). A rural alternative school and its effectiveness for preventing dropouts. *The Rural Educator, 25*(3), 25-29.

Johnston, B. J., & Wetherill, K. S. (1998). HSJ special issue introduction -- Alternative schooling. *The High School Journal, 81*(4), 177-182.

Jones, J.N. (2011). Narratives of student engagement in an alternative learning context. *Journal of Education for Students Placed at Risk (JESPAR), 16*(3), 219-236.   http://dx.doi.org/10.1080/10824669.2011.586299

Kellmayer, J. (1995). *How to establish an alternative school.* Thousand Oaks, CA: Corwin Press, Inc

Kelly, D.M. (1993). *Last chance high: How girls and boys drop in and out of alternative schools.* New Haven, CT: Yale University Press.

Kennedy, R.L. & Morton, J.H. (1999). *A school for healing: Alternative strategies for teaching at-risk students.* New York, NY: Peter Lang International Academic Publishers.

Kim, J-H. (2011): Narrative inquiry into (re)imagining alternative schools: A case study of Kevin Gonzales. *International Journal of Qualitative Studies in Education, 24*(1), 77-96.

Kim, J., & Taylor, K. A. (2008). Rethinking alternative education to break the cycle of educational inequality and inequity. *Journal of Educational Research, 101*(4), 207-219.

Kleiner, B., Porch, R., and Farris, E. (2002). *Public Alternative Schools and Programs for Students At-risk of Education Failure: 2000–01* (NCES 2002–004). U.S. Department of Education. Washington, DC: National Center for Education Statistics.

Kubik, M. Y., Lytle, L. & Fulkerson, J. A. (2004). Physical activity, dietary practices, and other health behaviors of at-risk youth attending alternative high schools. *Journal of School Health, 74*, 119–124. doi: 10.1111/j.1746-1561.2004.tb06613.x

Kvale, S. (1996). *InterViews: An introduction to qualitative research interviewing.* Thousand Oaks, CA: Sage Publications.

Kvale, S. (1994). Ten standard objections to qualitative research interviews. *Journal of Phenomenological Psychology, 25*(2), 147-171.

Kvale, S. (1983). The qualitative research interview: A phenomenological and hermeneutical mode of understanding. *Journal of Phenomenological Psychology, 14*(2), 171-196.

Lagana-Riordan, C., Aguilar, J.P., Franklin, C., Streeter, C.L., Kim, J.S., Tripodi, S.J. & Hopson. L.M. (2011). At-risk students' perceptions of traditional schools and a solution-focused public alternative school. *Preventing School Failure: Alternative Education for Children and Youth, 55*(3), 105-114.

Lange, C. M. (1998). Characteristics of alternative schools and programs serving at-risk students. *The High School Journal, 81*(4) 183-198.

Lange, C.M. & Lehr, C.A. (1999). At-risk students attending second chance programs: Measuring performance in desired outcome domains. *Journal of Education for Students Placed at Risk (JESPAR), 4*(2), 173-192.

Lange, C.M. & Sletten, S.J. (2002). *Alternative education: A brief history and research synthesis.* Alexandria, VA: National Association of State Directors of Special Education

Larson, S. (2005a). Connecting with youth in crisis. *Reclaiming Children and Youth, 14*(2), 87-90.

Larson, S. (2005b). Teaching for transformation in today's challenging youth. *Reclaiming Children and Youth, 14*(1), 27-31.

Laursen, E. K. (2005). Rather than fixing kids -- Build positive peer cultures. *Reclaiming Children and Youth, 14*(3), 137-142.

Lehr, C. A., & Lange, C. M. (2003). Alternative schools serving students with and without disabilities: What are the current issues and challenges? *Preventing School Failure: Alternative Education for Children and Youth, 47*(2), 59-65.

Lehr, C.A., Tan, C.S., & Ysseldyke. J. (2009). Alternative schools: A synthesis of state-level policy and research. *Remedial and Special Education, 30,* 19-32. doi:10.1177/0741932508315645

Leone, P.E. & Drakeford, W. (1999). Alternative Education: From a "Last Chance" to a Proactive Model. *The Clearing House: A Journal of Educational Strategies, Issues and Ideas, 73*(2), 86-88

Lesley's Coffee Spot. (2012). The starfish story. Retrieved from http://lesleyscoffeestop.blogspot.ca/2012/07/starfish-story.html

Lichtman, M. (2010). Qualitative research in education: A user's guide. (2nd ed.). Thousand Oaks, CA: Sage Publications.

Long, C., Page, J., Hail, B., Davis, T., & Mitchell, L. (2003). Community mental health-- In an alternative school, in the public schools, and in the kitchen! *Reclaiming Children and Youth, 11*(4), 231-235.

McCall, H.J. (2003). When successful alternative students "disengage" from regular school. *Reclaiming Children and Youth, 12*(2), 113-117.

McGee, J. (2001). Reflections of an alternative school administrator. *The Phi Delta Kappan, 82*(8), 588-591.

McNulty, C.P. & Roseboro, D.L. (2009): "I'm not really that bad": Alternative School Students, Stigma, and Identity Politics. *Equity & Excellence in Education, 42*(4), 412-427.

Magee-Quinn, M., Poirier, J.M., Faller, S.E., Gable, R.A. & Tonelson, S.W. (2006). An examination of school climate in effective alternative programs. *Preventing School Failure: Alternative Education for Children and Youth, 51*(1), 11-17.

Martin, E.J., Tobin, T.J. & Sugai, G.M. (2003). Current Information on Dropout Prevention: Ideas from Practitioners and the Literature. *Preventing School Failure: Alternative Education for Children and Youth, 47*(1), 10-17

Maslow, A.H. (1987). *Motivation and Personality* (3rd ed.). New York, NY: Harper & Row, Publishers Inc.

Mertens, D. M. (2005). *Research and evaluation in education and psychology: Integrating diversity with quantitative, qualitative, and mixed methods* (2nd ed.). Thousand Oaks, CA: Sage Publications.

151

Meyers, A. (1988). Examining alternative education over the past thirty years. *Education, 109*(1), 76-81.

Miles, M. B., & Huberman, A. M. (1994). *Qualitative data analysis: An expanded sourcebook* (2nd ed.). Thousand Oaks, CA: Sage Publications.

Morrissette, P. (2011). Exploring student experiences within the alternative high school context. *Canadian Journal of Education, 34*(2), 169-188.

Moustakas, C. E. (1994). *Phenomenological research methods*. Thousand Oaks, CA: Sage Publications.

Neufeld, G. & Maté, G. (2004). *Hold onto your kids: Why parents need to matter more than peers*. Vancouver, BC: Vintage Canada Random House.

Nicholson, D. & Artz, S. (2008). *Education for At-risk Youth: Have we moved away from the* alternatives *movement and to what effects?* Submitted to the Human Early Learning Partnership Program, Vancouver, BC.

Oden, S. (1995). Studying youth programs to assess influences on youth development: New roles for researchers. *Journal of Adolescent Research, 10*(1), 173-186. doi:10.1177/0743554895101010

Olive, E. (2003). The North Star model of alternative education. *Reclaiming Children and Youth, 12*(2), 98.

Owens, L., & Konkol, L. (2004). Transitioning from alternative to traditional school settings: A student perspective. *Reclaiming Children and Youth, 13*(3), 173-176.

Patton, M. Q. (2002). *Qualitative research & evaluation methods* (3rd ed.). Thousand Oaks, CA: Sage Publications.

Payne, R. (1996). A framework for understanding poverty. (4th ed.). Highlands, TX: aha! Process Inc.

Phillips, G. L. (1992). *Classroom rituals for at-risk learners.* Vancouver, BC: EduServ Inc.

Platt, J.S., Casey, R.E. & Faessel, R.T. (2006). The need for a paradigmatic change in juvenile correctional education. *Preventing School Failure: Alternative Education for Children and Youth, 51*(1), 31-38.

Powell, D. E. (2003). Demystifying alternative education: Considering what really works. *Reclaiming Children and Youth, 12*(2), 68-70.

Poyrazli, S., Ferrer-Wreder, L., Meister, D.G., Forthun, L., Coatsworth, J.D. & Graham. K.M. (2008). Academic achievement, employment, age and gender and students' experience of alternative school. *Adolescence, 43*(171), 547-556.

Prein, G., Bird, K., & Kelle, U. (1995). *Computer-aided qualitative data analysis: Theory, methods and practice.* Thousand Oaks, CA: Sage Publications.

Premier's Technology Council. (2010*): A vision for 21st century education.* Retrieved from: http://www.gov.bc.ca/premier/attachments/PTC_vision%20for_education. pdf.

Raywid, M. A. (2006). Themes that serve schools well. *Phi Delta Kappan, 87*(9), 654-656.

Raywid, M. A. (2001). What to do with students who are not succeeding. *The Phi Delta Kappan, 82*(8), 582-584.

Raywid, M. A. (1997). *Small schools: A reform that works: An occasional paper of the small schools coalition.* Chicago, IL: Small Schools Coalition.

Raywid, M. A. (1996). *Taking stock: The movement to create mini-schools, schools-within-schools, and separate small schools. Urban diversity series*

153

no. 108. Madison, WI: Center on Organization and Restructuring of Schools.

Raywid, M. A. (1994). Alternative schools: The state of the art. *Educational Leadership, 52*(1), 26-31.

Raywid, M. A. (1983). Alternative schools as a model for public education. *Theory into Practice, 22*(3), 190-97.

Raywid, M.A. (1982). The current status of schools of choice in public secondary education. *Project on Alternatives in Education.* Hempstead, NY: Hofstra University.

Raywid, M. A. (1981). The first decade of public school alternatives. *The Phi Delta Kappan, 62*(8), pp. 551-554.

Reed, R. (2011). Connecting with a disconnected student. *Reclaiming Children and Youth, 20*(1), 51-53.

Richardson, L. & St-Pierre, E. (2005). Writing: A method of inquiry. In N.K. Denzin, & Y.S. Lincoln, (eds.), *The SAGE handbook of qualitative research* (3nd ed., pp. 959-978). Thousand Oaks, CA: Sage Publications.

Rix, J., & Twining, P. (2007). Exploring education systems: Towards a typology for future learning? *Educational Research, 49*(4), 329-341.

Sagor, R. (2006). Alternative programs for at-risk students: Wolves in sheep's clothing? *CYC-Online Reading for Child and Youth Care People, 89,* 1–9.

Sagor, R. (1999). Equity and excellence in public schools: The role of the alternative school. *The Clearing House: A Journal of Educational Strategies, Issues and Ideas, 73*(2), 72-75. doi:10.1080/00098659909600150.

San Martin, T.L. & Calabrese, R.L. (2011). Empowering at-risk students through appreciative inquiry. *International Journal of Educational Management, 25*(2), 110 – 123.

Sandberg, J. (2005). How do we justify knowledge produced within interpretive approaches? *Organizational Research Methods, 8*(1), 41-68. doi:10.1177/1094428104272000

Saunders, J. A., & Saunders, E. J. (2002). Alternative school students' perceptions of past [traditional] and current [alternative] school environments. *The High School Journal, 85*(2), 12-23.

Schnoes, C., Reid, R., Wagner, M., & Marper, C. (2006). ADHD among students receiving special education services: A national survey. *Exceptional Children, 72*(4), 483-496.

Schwandt, T. A. (2002). *Evaluation practice reconsidered.* New York: Peter Lang.

Schwandt, T.A. (2000). Three epistemological stances for qualitative inquiry: Interpretivism, hermeneutics and social constructionsim. In N.K. Denzin, & Y.S. Lincoln, (eds.), *The SAGE handbook of qualitative research* (2nd ed., pp. 189-213). Thousand Oaks, CA: Sage Publications.

Seita, J. (2010). Missing data: Discovering the private logic of adult-wary youth. *Reclaiming Children and Youth, 19*(2), 51-54.

Shank, G. (2006). Six alternatives to mixed methods in qualitative research. *Qualitative Research in Psychology, 3*(4), 346-356. doi:10.1177/1478088706070842

Shank, G. (1994). Shaping qualitative research in educational psychology. *Contemporary Educational Psychology, 19*(3), 340-359. doi:10.1006/ceps.1994.1025

Shank, G. & Villella, O. (2004). Building on new foundations: Core principles and new directions for qualitative research. *The Journal of Educational Research, 98*(1), 46-55.

Shirley, D.S. (2010). Evaluation of at-risk students' needs in public alternative schools. (unpublished doctoral dissertation). Phoenix, AZ: Argosy University/Online.

Smith , A., Peled, M. Albert, M., Mackay, L., Stewart, D., Saewyc, E., & the McCreary Center Society. (2007). *Making the grade: A review of alternative education programs in British Columbia.* Vancouver, BC: McCreary Center Society.

Smith, G. R., Gregory, T. B., & Pugh, R. C. (1981). Meeting student needs: Evidence for the superiority of alternative schools. *The Phi Delta Kappan, 62*(8), 561-564.

Struchen, W. & Porta, M. (1997). From role-modeling to mentoring for African American youth: Ingredients for successful relationships. *Preventing School Failure: Alternative Education for Children and Youth, 41*(3), 119-123.

Tissington, L.D. (2006). History: Our hope for the future. *Preventing School Failure: Alternative Education for Children and Youth, 51*(1), 19-25.

Tissington, L. D., & Grow, A. (2007). Alternative certified teachers and children at- risk. *Preventing School Failure: Alternative Education for Children and Youth, 51* (2), 23-27.

Tobin, T. & Sprague, J. (2000). Alternative education strategies: Reducing violence in school and the community. *Journal of Emotional and Behavioral Disorders, 8*(3), 177-186. doi:10.1177/106342660000800305.

Vadeboncoeur, J. A. (2009). Spaces of difference: The contradictions of alternative educational programs. *Educational Studies, 45*(3), 280-299. doi:10.1080/00131940902910974

Van Acker, R. (2007). Antisocial, aggressive, and violent behavior in children and adolescents within alternative education settings: *Preventing School Failure: Alternative Education for Children and Youth, 51*(2), 5-12.

VanderVen, K. (2004). Adults are still needed! Intergenerational and mentoring activities. *Reclaiming Children and Youth, 13*(2), 94-102.

Watson, S. M., Westby, C. E., & Gable, R. A. (2007). A framework for addressing the needs of students prenatally exposed to alcohol and other drugs. *Preventing School Failure, Alternative Education for Children and Youth, 52*(1), 25-32.

Weitzman, E.A. (2000). Software and Qualitative Research. In N.K. Denzin, & Y.S. Lincoln, (eds.), *The SAGE handbook of qualitative research* (2nd ed., pp. 803-820). Thousand Oaks, CA: Sage Publications.

Wilkins, J. (2007). School characteristics that influence student attendance: Experiences of students in a school avoidance program. *The High School Journal, 91*(3), 12-30.

Wolf, E.M. & Wolf, D.A. (2008). Mixed results in a transitional planning program for alternative school students. *Evaluation Review, 32*(2), 187-215. doi:10.1177/0193841X07310600

Wood, M.M. (2001). Viewpoint: Preventing school failure: A teacher's current conundrum. *Preventing School Failure: Alternative Education for Children and Youth, 45*(2), 52-57.

Young, T. (1990). *Public alternative education: Options and choice for today's schools.* New York, NY: Teachers College Press.

Zhang, K.C. (2008). Through new lens: Young adolescent girls' perceptions of their school experience in an alternative education program. *International Journal of Special Education, 23*(2), 96-100.

Zweig, J.M. (2003). *Vulnerable Youth: Identifying their need for alternative education settings.* Washington, D.C.: The Urban Institute.

APPENDIX A

Interview questions

1. How long have you been in education?
    a. As a support worker?
    b. As a teacher?
    c. As an administrator?
2. How long were you in:
    a. Mainstream schools?
    b. Alternative education?
3. What brought you to alternative education? (Event? Vocation?)
    a. Do these reasons still stand today?
4. What specialized training were you offered in order to enhance your effectiveness in alternative education?
5. What professional development did you pursue to enhance your effectiveness in alternative education?
6. In general, what changes have you seen in education over the years?
    a. Are these changes also reflected in alternative education?
    b. Would you say that these changes have been at the:
        i. Ideological level?   Political level?   Program level? Pedagogical?
        ii. Characteristics of the student population?
7. What philosophy and/or framework guide your work in alternative education?
8. What approach do you believe is most effective in working with vulnerable youth and families in an alternative setting?
9. What are you hoping to accomplish in working with this student population?

a. Is it outcome-driven, such as:

    i. Graduation?

    ii. Vocational training/work experience?

    iii. Transitioning back to mainstream?

b. Or is it process-driven, such as:

    i. Developing basic life-skills?

    ii. Connecting with community-based services?

    iii. Developing a capable citizen?

10. How would you:

    a. Describe an effective alternative education program?

    b. Define 'success' in an alternative education program?

11. What do you see as alternative education's greatest strength?

    a. In this district specifically?

12. What do you believe is needed in order to enhance alternative education services?

    a. In this district specifically?

13. What is your take on the 21st Century personalized learning paradigm?

    a. Its impact on the delivery of mainstream education?

    b. Its impact on the delivery of alternative education?

    c. Do you see this 21st Century learning paradigm as bridging or widening the gap between mainstream and alternative education?

14. What advice do you have to offer the BC Ministry of Education with regards to enhancing alternative education services?

15. Is there anything important you feel we have not discussed regarding alternative education?

16. Is there anything else you would like to add before we end this recording?

Printed by
Schaltungsdienst Lange o.H.G., Berlin